Code Brown

13 Humorous True-Life Tales
About Poop (Yes, Poop)

Edited by Garrett Calcaterra

DEDICATION

To my family and friends who instilled in me the wisdom of not taking oneself too seriously, especially my father Paul Calcaterra. Additional thanks to Corine Calcaterra, Shirley Phillips, Biff Phillips, Mandy Burke, and the Kempters, without whom this book would not exist.

CONTENTS

ACKNOWLEDGMENTS

This book would not have been possible if it were not for the hard work and dedication of all the contributors to *Code Brown*, not only the authors in this final edition, but also those who contributed to the larger, unpublished version. I'd like to thank all of them, along with The Biscuits, The Wordmongers, Chris Turk, and my agent Elizabeth Kracht.

INTRODUCTION:
DEATH, TAXES, AND SHIT

Garrett Calcaterra

IT IS A LITTLE KNOWN FACT that there are three types of muscle in the human body. *Skeletal muscle* is the one most people think of when they think muscle. It's the muscle-type that fills out our bodies and moves our appendages around: our biceps, triceps, quadriceps, and yes, our gluteus maximus. *Cardiac muscle* is another well-known one. It's the muscle our heart is made of. It keeps blood pumping through our bodies year after year, decade after decade, until one day it finally craps out. The lesser known of the three muscle tissue types is *smooth muscle*. Smooth muscle is the tissue that makes our arteries expand and contract, and it is also the tissue that keeps things moving along through our intestinal tract, sort of like how your fingers work the last bit of toothpaste out of the toothpaste tube. I learned all this back in my college days, before I decided to become a science fiction and fantasy author, when I was getting my degree in chemistry and biology, still thinking I would get a proper job as an optometrist.

"Smooth muscle gets no respect," my anatomy professor

told my class one day. "It does not have the sheer brute strength of skeletal muscle, nor does it reside in the ever glamorous heart. However, similar to cardiac muscle, smooth muscle does not fatigue. The smooth muscle in our intestines, for example, will continue to push and push without stopping, until the day we die (and even then, for another hour or two). Meanwhile, our anal sphincter is comprised of skeletal muscle. This little spiral-shaped muscle is intensely strong; it can hold the gates against a furious attack, but like all skeletal muscle it will eventually grow tired. It can only withstand the siege of stools for so long. Eventually, inevitably, we must poop."

This lecture has stuck with me all these years, mostly I assumed, because it was funny to hear an older gentleman with a Ph.D. and a very distinguished lisp talk about poop. But I'm not so sure anymore. Now, in the zenith of my adulthood, I've grown up a little and I've come to realize that this speech—of unrelenting smooth muscle, of the inevitability of shitting—is in fact the perfect metaphor for human existence.

Think about it. Defecating is as natural as breathing and eating, yet because of the foul appearance and gag-inducing smell, we choose to ignore its existence. In polite company, we instinctively pretend like we don't hear the flatulent noises coming from the bathroom down the hallway. We pretend like we don't smell the nose-curling stench, or see the greasy skid marks left on the inside of the toilet bowl. We don't dare point a finger at anyone else because we know at any given moment the table will be turned and we will be the person chumming up the toilet with half-digested corn kernels that refuse to flush.

But why so much denial? Who is it we think we're fooling? We know shitting is natural, inevitable, that resistance is futile, and yet, like little sphincters, we keep up the façade. Why is it we hide our bowel movements from even our lovers, the ones who see our naked bodies and share our most intimate of acts?

I'll tell you why. It's because shit is king. Not a proper king, mind you. More like a king in modern Spain or England—a symbolic figurehead of all our insecurities, all the embarrassing personal qualities we keep secret. Cellulite, debilitating bad breath, deviant sexual thoughts, irrational fears, addictions, ineptness at calculating tips... we keep these things secret and guard them like they're our very soul, and the irony is, each and every one of us has insecurities and embarrassing characteristics. Just like all of us shit.

Think I'm wrong? Take a look at our idioms.

Shit happens.

Up shit creek.

What a shitty day.

Shit-eating grin.

Screw you, shithead!

Oh shit...

Luckily, people with a sense of humor have more or less figured this all out. There's nothing that can be done about the truly shitty things in our lives, so it's best to not take ourselves too seriously and instead have a good laugh at our own expense. This is why once the deed is done, the inherent mishaps involved with shitting are fodder for our greatest yarns and barroom jokes. Whether you accidentally splotched your underwear right before a big board meeting, got the trots while on a twelve-hour plane ride, or ran into the opposite sex's restroom at a fancy restaurant because you had to crap so bad you couldn't see straight, these are the stories we tell when in good company and in need of a hearty laugh. And that's where this book comes in.

Code Brown first took life at the dinner table with my extended family after Thanksgiving dinner a few years back. For whatever reason, my dad, my step-mom, my cousins, my uncles, an aunt or two, and I sat around telling embarrassing poop stories (I like to think this is because my family has a good sense of humor and doesn't take itself too seriously, not because we're sickos), and after a good thirty minutes of laughing so hard our sides ached, my dad said to me, "You know, you should write a book with all these stories in it." At first, I scoffed (as any grown man aught to do), but then I got to thinking. My dad was right. Life can be pretty shitty at times, and these are just the type of stories people need to hear to lighten things up. So, I agreed. I made it my mission to seek out the funniest true-life pooping stories and essays about shit the world has ever seen, and after many years and sorting through the shit, so to speak, here they are!

I hope the stories will make you laugh as hard as I did, because here's another thing I learned back in my college anatomy class: laughing is good for your health. It'll help you live longer, and while that entails more shitting and paying taxes, don't we all want to prolong the other, less desirable certainty in life....

-Garrett Calcaterra
November 2013

DRAINED

Jeffrey Wallace

I DIDN'T KNOW THIS before it happened but there's something about lying flat on my back in a gauzy hospital gown that makes me fall in love with everyone, especially the women in white who traipse in to check my chart in the shadows of night and touch me and give me another armload of opiates if I simply lie when they ask me, "on a scale of one to ten, how much pain…." If I'd known burning a hole in my colon would put me in this position, in a bed with smiling nurses and a remote control and an endless string of euphoric highs, you think I wouldn't have hurt myself sooner? Think again.

This is the story I was telling my friend Carl. Our families had met for a weekend at the beach, and as our wives and kids played in the surf, Carl seemed to be bothered by something. I've known him long enough to know when something's nagging at him, and by the way he was squinting and fingering his beer, I could see there was something about my story that didn't quite satisfy him. Carl is a curious man.

"So okay," he said. "I get that part. But I still don't get the part about how you got there."

"I told you. My wife drove me to the emergency room."

"No, I mean how you got into a position where you needed to go."

"I told you. I burned a hole in my colon."

Carl squinted and looked away, out toward Catalina, and though he raised the lip of his beer bottle to his mouth, he merely tongued the hole. "Um hmm," he said in a way that made it clear he was still fishing for more.

I drank too, knowing full well what he was after. You can tell a guy everything you want him to know and he'll still want more. It's not the story a guy is after—it's the details. Carl wanted whatever it was I didn't want to explain.

"Okay," he said, still not looking at me. "But how the hell does somebody burn a hole in their colon, exactly? How the hell… you know?"

Carl is bowel-centric, anal retentive by nature. He makes more "up the butt" cracks than anyone I've ever known. He also suspects the worst in people. Especially his friends. In short: Carl suspected me of something unmanly.

"How the hell does anyone do that?" he said, as if he couldn't guess. "How does someone even get anything near their colon?"

"It ain't easy, I suppose," I said.

My wife's voice rose above the din of the crashing surf. It sounded good, thirty yards distant.

"I don't suppose it is," he said, looking right at me and raising one brow.

"You don't want to know," I said, letting him dangle. "Trust me."

"Now I want to know even more."

"No you don't."

"Yes I do."

"It's embarrassing."

"Even better."

He grabbed the rusting handle at the side of his beach chair and leaned back. The little umbrella shaded his greasy legs from the tropical sun.

"Tell me," he said, fully prone. "Or maybe I'll have to ask

6

your wife."

***

On my second night in the hospital an old man was moved into the bed on the other side of my room. A little curtain separated us from seeing each other but not from hearing every groan and breath. His wife spent the whole day at his side feeding him crackers she boasted of swiping from the cafeteria, and every time she came in or out of the room, she had to pass by the foot of my bed. I smiled the first time or two, being stoned and roommates and all, but instead of smiling back or offering a cracker or crumb of kindness, that old permed twig slowed down just enough to glare and study me as if I were a traffic accident, the details of which she'd report dutifully to her constipated husband.

"He still has his lunch tray," she'd tell him. Or, "he's just watching TV." I remember she sounded disappointed. "He looks fine to me."

After the first few times of smiling and receiving nothing in return I started making faces. This at least gave her something more to be angry about than the doctor's inattention to her husband.

"Ignore him," the man said. This guy was what... eight, maybe ten feet away from me? "Who cares about him?"

On the third day a specialist introduced himself and looked me over and asked about my pain, and he pressed on me and made me lift my gown and, after snapping on a rubber glove, went spelunking. I watched a reflection of the Cubs' game on the surface of the x-ray panel mounted above my bed as he tended to business. A few minutes after the doctor left, my favorite daytime nurse appeared. She had a well-placed mole and a nametag I could never read because it rested at such a steep slope on her breast. She set down a coil of rubber and two gallon-jugs on my food tray. When I asked what those were for she uttered a one word reply, without apology.

"Enema."

"Oh my God," whispered the woman from behind the curtain. "Not in here."

7

***

How's a man supposed to feel when the woman he's fantasized about for three days and nights tells him she's going to make him drop his pants and roll over? A little fondling I could handle… but an enema? I've never had an enema, never fantasized about having an enema, never wanted to fantasize about having one. Call me old fashioned, call it boundary issues, blame my father… say whatever you want but keep that coil of rubber tubing away from me and my private little friend, the one I feel guilty about just for washing. So thoroughly.

The drugs coursing through my veins dulled the pain but not the fear. "Is that really necessary?" I said, softly. "Can't we do something else?"

She gently placed her hand on my arm and whispered something about how eager the doctor was to see "what's going on in there." She added something poetic about how this cleansing was required in order to see, like on a clear day, what my insides really looked like on the big screen down in radiology. Then she left.

*** .

On the beach, Carl continued to press. He reminded me of several "personally embarrassing" things he'd told me over the years, stupid things, ordinary things, adding with each disclosure a little huff to his tone to indicate a lack of reciprocity on my part. "What's the big deal, anyway?" he said. "If you shoved something up your ass, you really think I care?"

"I didn't shove anything up my ass, Carl," I said, flicking moisture from my bottle at him.

"Sure," he said. "Of course not. But I saw a thing on the Internet about how this guy in Chicago stuck a flashlight—"

"I was taking painkillers, okay? I'd had surgery on my shoulder and my idiot doctor didn't say anything about the side effects. Seriously."

"You're telling me pain killers burned a hole in your colon? I don't think so."

I heard one of his bratty kids screaming down by the water but we both ignored it.

8

"The truth shall set you free, my friend," he chirped, covering his face with a magazine. "Shit it out for me."

***

If you've never had an enema let me say only this: it's a fairly straightforward procedure that involves funneling, squeezing, a well-placed bucket, and a series of simple commands. Some people find this entertaining. I will never be one of them.

When my nurse returned I was sitting up. I had spent the last half hour arranging the words of my request just-so, and I delivered them flawlessly. "Could someone else do the procedure?"

She responded with a question and crossing of the arms—I could tell she was offended. Too bad. It was a price I had to pay. She left again, only this time with no parting words of encouragement. Just this: "I'll check with Juanita."

***

Carl continued to explore the alleged relationship between painkillers and colons and I could see that without explanation I'd never enjoy the scenery.

"Listen. The doctor said I could take one every four to six hours," I told him. "So that's what I did. I took one every four hours."

"And?"

"And I did that for weeks."

"You do love your drugs."

"Yeah, but not the side effects. After forty days and forty nights I was... higher and drier and more compacted than a cement mixer stranded in the outback."

He laughed. I felt entertaining. Who knew bowel movements, or lack thereof, could be so amusing?

"And then one night after watching an old *Star Trek* episode with my son... you know the one where the lady turns into the salt monster?"

"Yeah."

"I went to the bathroom. And I pushed and I pushed and I pushhhhhhhhed and I puuuuusssssshhhhhhhhheddddddddd—"

9

"I get it."

"Ever hear some guy in the airport pushing like that? Jeez. It kills me when I hear that now. People have no idea. You can really damage your innards."

"Stay on topic. You were pushing…"

"Like you wouldn't believe. I was determined, man. I'm telling you."

The waves crashed against the sand. Carl sipped his beer and nodded.

"I never pushed so hard in my fucking life," I said.

Carl added a few grunting noises and strained facial gestures. That's the kind of friend he is.

"You look a little like Captain Kirk right now," I told him. He thanked me and asked what happened next.

"Well, the pushing worked. I did what I hadn't done in weeks… except I also had myself a shitload of blood."

"Nice."

"Right. Off we went to the emergency room."

Carl didn't answer. A hoard of MILFs was emerging from the surf. Wet, laughing, and all wearing sunscreen. He reached for his binoculars. I looked too. One of the women emerged from the surf in slow motion, shaking her hair from side to side, reminding me of someone I once knew.

***

Nurse Juanita was a five-foot Filipino fireplug. Black hair, white teeth, man-hands and an attitude that left no room for nonsense. "I am Juanita," she said. "It's time for your enema. Roll over, please." She snatched the tubing off my tray and shook it loose until it dangled like a snake. From a hidden pocket she withdrew a creased tube of lube.

I introduced myself by rolling over. A small mirror on the wall gave me a great view of myself. Thirty seconds after meeting, Juanita had lifted my gown and exposed my buttocks and slapped a glob of lubricant in place with a finger that never hesitated, a finger that moved like an arrow, burrowing itself into the bullseye.

"Cold," I said.

"Yes."

"They're giving it in here," said the woman behind the curtain. Her husband was quiet. I appreciated that.

Juanita, the professional enemizer. She had it down, not a wasted motion in sight. She read me my rights, gave me my orders, plugged me in and said, in a thick accent that reminded me of a moist Manila morning, "What you have to do is hold it until you can't stand it anymore. And when you can't stand it, hold it a little more. Don't go until I say go. Understand?"

The fluids were already making their way inside. Yes, yes I understood. I also understood how it must feel to be the new kid on the cell block. I grabbed a handful of starched sheet and squeezed.

"Hold it," she said. "We have another pint to go yet."

Another pint? I thought of beer. I thought of England. There's no sensation like the one that comes with being filled like a balloon.

"I need to go," I said, gritting my teeth.

"No. You can hold it."

For several moments the only sound was that of Juanita moving things around. I kept my face pressed against the bed, squeezing and biting the pillow. When the curtain dividing the room rustled, I saw the reflection of the old lady peeking at me from behind, wide-eyed. I was beyond the point of caring.

"Ahhh," I groaned. "Am I full yet? This…is…hard…"

"Not yet," Juanita cried. "Almost." She started chanting: "Hold it. Hold it. Hold it. Hold it…"

"How much more?"

"Not much. I tell you when."

Things grew blurry. I'd never in all my life put so much concentration on holding something that wanted to move. "I gotta go I gotta go," I said, and for the first time I thought about what would happen if I lost control.

"Hold it!" Juanita shouted. "Not yet!"

"It's hard…"

"Hold hold hold hold!"

"What's he holding?" said the man behind the curtain.

Again the curtain parted and two beady eyes glared at my backside.

"Now!" I cried. "Please!"

"Hold-hold-hold!" Juanita barked, slapping my love handle. "Almost there!"

***

Back on the beach, Carl had what he needed. He was nodding as I finished my story, nodding and smiling—relieved a little too, I think, to believe me. As soon as I finished my story he launched straight into one of his own, one of those "that reminds me" stories, a story about how he'd poked a hole in a waterbed when he was kid, and about how that stream of stinky warm water spurted up and out across the room like a fountain. "You wouldn't believe it!" he said, "I swear, it went, like, fifteen feet!"

"Oh, I believe it," I said. "Trust me. I believe it."

WHAT'S ON THE INSIDE

Lisa Hallsted

MY BROTHER LOVES HIS ANUS. Not in a what's-your-sexual-orientation type of way. Just in the way that all boys love their buttholes. Pooping, farting, diarrhea, butt slapping, pulling down pants in public. Both one's own, as well as the pants of others, to enrich the lives of friends, girlfriends, passengers in cars, entire school assemblies, and of course, sisters. Christopher once waited a good fifteen minutes with his ass hanging out, bent over in our entryway, his butt facing the front door, poised to welcome me home from work. He was home from college one summer, we were both living at home, and he heard my car pull up. It took fifteen minutes because, being a girl, that's about the length of time it took me to park, put lipstick and cigarettes back in my purse, get out of the car, grab a shopping bag from the back, walk to the front door, dig for the keys, put down the shopping bag, dig some more, pet the cat, and fiddle with the lock. Christopher waited. He waited with the patience of Prometheus. And, if you ask him, he'll tell you it was worth it. Because BA-ing your older sister is a little like stealing fire from the gods, and baring your bowels to the sky is simply the price you pay for progress. I opened the door and screamed, dropped the shopping bag, tossed the purse, and almost stepped on the cat while staggering back from the full fruit basket that Christopher had hung in mid-air. Yes, it was a fruit basket. And if you don't know what that means, look it up on Urban Dictionary.

But I digress. This story is about poop, and my brother's close personal relationship to it. My theory is that, for boys in general, the fascination starts with farts. Lighting them on fire, farting the alphabet, forming words. I hear that a quick search on YouTube will yield hundreds of videos dedicated to the art of farting on cue, and a male friend of mine once waxed poetic for thirty minutes on the similarities between fart sounds and shoes. Boot-boot. High-heel. Shoooo. I'm almost jealous. In our formative years, girls are too preoccupied with lipstick, handbags, and shopping to take the time to get in touch with our intestines. (Though I can tell tampon stories that will make even my brother cringe.) Girls rarely realize the joys of competing for the stinkiest fart, and are often too body-conscious to even think about pulling down our pants in public. We are primed as targets for little brothers and their baskets. From the get go, women's weakness is externals. And men—well, early on, they know it's all about what's inside.

Which brings me to Christopher and Brian. Brian is one of my brother's best friends. Our mothers knew each other when they were pregnant, so technically they've been friends since the womb. They were dragged to church together, went all the way from first grade through high school together, partied together, and of course, burped and farted together. Naturally, they were roommates in college. I don't know much about Brian's seminal experiences with poop, but I do know that he once picked a booger so tremendous that he carried it on the tip of his finger all the way across their college campus, from biology to the dorm room, in order to show Chris.

It was their freshman year. Brian was pre-med, and Christopher hadn't landed on a major yet. He waffled awhile in the humanities—literature, history, philosophy—and eventually decided to spend a semester in France. I'm sure Brian was happy for him, but he also felt a tinge of jealousy.

Perhaps it was his course load. Perhaps he'd miss his friend. Whatever it was, Christopher's departure was the moment Brian uttered one of the more famous quotes in the pantheon of my brother's poo stories.

"You know," Brian said, "all my friends go to Europe and nobody ever sends me shit."

"I'll send you something," Chris said, and he still swears that, at the time, he was only thinking a t-shirt or an Eiffel Tower keychain.

But inspiration struck about halfway through his stay. Chris and two other boys were guests of a family living outside of Paris. After weeks of eating nothing but French bread and cheese, combined with the abundant quantities of beer and wine that American college students typically consume on their first trip to Europe, Christopher knew that he could send Brian something special. The boys rooted around in the kitchen and were delighted to discover that their French hosts stocked the equivalent of Saran Wrap. A Ziploc, of course, would have been better, with its superior shelf life and ability to "Lock in Freshness!" but time was short, it was dark, and they didn't want to get caught.

The logistics were tough. There were variables to account for—mass, volume, stability. Chris didn't want to stretch the Saran Wrap under the seat. It might break, or slip down into the toilet. Picking your own poo out of the toilet water seemed a bit much. The plan was disgusting, but it didn't have to be messy. He thought about doing the ergonomic squat, and foregoing the toilet entirely. Crouching low, cupping his Saran-wrapped hand under his asshole and catching the turd like a groundball. But then he got creative. He closed the lid of the toilet, stretched the plastic tight across the top, balanced his butt in the air, and took a dump on the cold, hard surface. And it worked. The shit held together, it didn't roll off, and it was a respectable six or so inches. Christopher folded the plastic around the poo, sealed it up as best he could, and took it gently in his fist.

The plan was to mail it the next day. The boys put it in a

large shipping envelope and propped it up in the corner of their bedroom. By morning it stank. Their options were limited, so the entire package went into a second, heavier envelope that contained the smell well enough to ready it for public consumption.

I will admit there are moments in my brother's life when I have been horrified. But he has also made me proud. I am proud that he stuck with the humanities, all the way through to a Master's degree and now teaches English literature. I am glad I have a brother who flew all the way to Florida to help me move back to California. (He farted in the car through seven states and, in Tucson, had a bout of diarrhea so noxious we still talk about it at Christmas.) And I smile every time I think of Christopher, a large mailer under his arm, walking down some street in France, intent on sending a piece of his own shit through the international postal system.

Back at the dorm, Brian wasn't completely without suspicion. Before he left, Christopher had TP'd their room. Like. He really. TP'd their room. He didn't just whimsically toss around a few rolls. He attacked the room with vigor and attention to detail. Toilet paper was anchored to every immovable surface. There was TP in the drawers, TP stuffed in shirt sleeves, and TP between the sheets. Brian found bits of toilet paper in his underwear, hiding in pockets, and rolled in remote corners of the closet. Moreover, he wasn't convinced that toilet paper was the only memento Christopher had left behind. For months, Brian tensed and held his nose every time he pulled out a sock or reached into his desk.

In France, Chris waited in line at the post office. When he got to the counter he wrote "chocolate" across the front, handed it to the lady, and waited while she weighed it, hopeful that his poo might be manly enough to warrant extra postage. It didn't. But she took it without question. Not one suspicious sniff. Chris marveled a bit at the lack of awareness, but then shrugged it off. It did stink. But it was the 90s. And it was France. A time long before heightened international customs laws in a country not known for sharing America's obsession with antibacterial soap, odor-blocking body wash, and the germ-fighting power of Lysol.

It was also a time before cell phones, texting and email. An international phone call was a big deal. So, Chris didn't know how long it took for his poo to get there, if at all, until months later. But it did get there. That piece of poo traveled over 5,600 miles. It left Paris, crossed the Atlantic, traversed the entire continental United States, and was successfully delivered to the Sierra Towers Men's Residence Hall on the campus of La Sierra University in Riverside, California. Mr. Hankey would be proud.

In the telling, Christopher is always careful to point out that, over time, the poo would naturally start to sweat, causing moisture to slowly saturate the entire package. With a smile, he notes that, all along its journey, each person who touched the package undoubtedly walked away with a little piece of Christopher on their hands. By the time it reached the dorm, it was wet.

"Dude. Pick up your mail."

That's what the hall monitor said to Brian when he walked into the lobby. The package was too big to put in his mailbox, so it had been propped behind the front desk. He handed the package to Brian.

"Dude." The hall monitor reiterated.

Brian took the package between his thumb and index finger.

"Oh my god," he said, "I know what this is."

He didn't even look at the return address. These were roommates who routinely farted into plastic bottles in order to save the smell for later, and kept a square-foot space on their wall where they stuck all the significant boogers from the school year.

Brian put his hand over his nose.

"Omigod, I know what this is."

He hurried out of the lobby with the package between his fingers.

"Oh shit, I totally know what this is."

He broke into a run down the stairs outside the dorm and continued muttering as if it were a smell-neutralizing mantra.

"I know what this is. I know what this is."

He reached the dumpster…

"I know what this is."

…then tore open the package and took a peek…

"AWW SHIT. I KNEW IT."

…and then he threw it into the dumpster.

I don't know if Brian ever retaliated, but they're still friends. Brian went on to be a doctor and can now tell poo stories that are painful and awful and not funny at all. My brother still loves his butt. He runs marathons now. And he has grown into a man who values the difference between intestinal fortitude and intestinal gas. But of course, marathoners are known to occasionally lose control of their bowels, and I still see a twinkle in Christopher's eye every time he recounts the latest on someone who pooped their pants at the finish line. It hasn't happened to him yet. But he's training for a triathlon. So, there's still time.

NOT ONCE, BUT TWICE

Shannon Medisky

AS TWO STRAPPED-FOR-CASH COLLEGE STUDENTS, my husband, Jason, and I briefly shared an apartment with a roommate. Only problem was, we didn't like the roommate much. A problem made even larger by the fact that it was a very small apartment, and our only furniture was a bed, a dresser and a smallish TV. That said, we spent a lot—and I do mean a lot—of our time inside our bedroom. In an effort to minimize run-ins with said roommate, we even ate all our meals inside our tiny four walls. Yep, it was cozy.

But life inside a one-room cocoon can admittedly get kind of boring, not to mention lonely. So it wasn't long before Jason and I decided to expand our family. That's right, we wanted a little one. So we did as any other young couple would do: we adopted an adorable, tiny kitten. Our family—and our one-room home—would never be the same again.

Funny how not having money can sometimes make it easier to spend. And never more so than in the case of young, exhausted college students. We were certainly no exception. After one particularly long day of work and school, we decided to order a pizza, and, as was the case with each and every meal, eat it in our room. The Guido's delivery guy could not come soon enough. But no matter, we passed the time by collecting crumpled bills and spare change from around the room. On second thought, it was probably a very good thing it took him so long. It gave us time to scrap together a tip, too.

After a brief argument followed promptly by a game of rock, paper, scissors to determine who would actually leave the room to get the pizza and consequently brave a run-in with the roommate, Jason materialized with the hot pie in hand. Phew! Pizza? Check! Breadsticks? Check! Successfully braving the minefields of cursory, polite pleasantries between people who despise one another? Check!

Our newest addition to the family, however, also spied the grub, and it wasn't long at all before she was jumping at the side of the bed, digging her claws into the mattress and hanging on for dear life. Unable to actually make the entire trip up herself, she began screeching and crying in an effort to make her plight and hunger—no, demands—known. Seeing as this furry little family member was still our little secret and unbeknownst to our roommate, we were exceedingly quick to shut her up. So with one hand, Jason scooped her up, peeling her paws away from the comforter like Velcro, and threw her up on the bed beside us.

So there we sat. Jason and I sprawled out on our bed eating our favorite Italian pie, cheese with extra sauce, and the cat gnawing on a small piece of crust to keep her quiet. Ah, all was right with the world, at least for a few minutes anyway. But then, it happened. IT! The unthinkable, the unbelievable, the "it's so disgusting I can't believe I'm having to relive it by typing it" IT. And even as I do so, Jason currently stands behind me—years later—waging a new battle. Does he double over in fits of laughter or instead focus all his energy on fighting his natural gag reflex as he recalls the very same story? Leaving him to his own dilemma, I press forward in a personal confessional of sorts. In an effort to purge myself of this dirty little secret that will forever be part of my story, here's exactly how it, uh... went down.

Sometime in between using my napkin and grabbing

another slice of pizza, I noticed a small bit of sauce on the bed. Not wanting it to leave a stain nor waste any of the delicious sauce, I promptly took my finger, wiped it up and proceeded to lick it. Only it didn't taste like pizza sauce. In an effort to ensure it indeed wasn't pizza sauce, I began to smack my lips together and draw my tongue against the roof of my mouth. Heck, I even went in for more, spying yet another blob of the red stuff. After a second tasting, I decided to involve Jason in my current thought process.

"Uh, Jason? I don't think that was sauce I ate..."

Together, we turned to look at the cat that, as if on cue, jumped from the bed and headed towards her litter box, leaving a trail of bloody diarrhea behind her. We looked at each other, our eyes wide and our mouths silent, as we began to piece together what it was I had just done, what I had just ate. And not once, but TWICE!

"No, no, you didn't!" Jason began to shout as he leapt from the bed. He proceeded to jump around the room, flailing his arms in the air shouting, "Ew! Ew!" I, on the other hand, was so stunned by the realization that I sat perfectly still on the bed, the pizza still next to me and the offending taste still thick inside my mouth.

"How? Why?" Jason began to sputter, still jumping up and down around the room in a dance of disgust. "And why are you still sitting there?"

His question was a rational one. Why was I still sitting there? The only conclusion I could come to then and even now, years later, is that somehow sitting there, I was able to deny what I had just done. Eat bloody cat diarrhea? And not once, but twice? Oh, no I didn't. I couldn't have. But the evidence still lingered inside my mouth. And no matter how hard I tried to forget or deny it, Jason's continual dance of disbelief wouldn't let me. Actually, if truth be told, by this point, he had hit the wall with a thud and slid to the floor in a fit of laughter.

Like an uncomfortable memory you can't erase from your mind's eye, no amount of Listerine seemed to completely clean my mouth, at least not enough for Jason to come near it again for a good long while. And kitty? Well, let's just say Jason couldn't look at her again without laughing and I—never again—used my fingers or my mouth to clean up anything.

SEPTIC

Michael Williams

A WEEK IS A LONG TIME to live without a formal toilet of some kind, especially in Colorado in the middle of February. What we had instead of a toilet was five acres of private property. Most of it was weedy pasture, sage flat, and juniper thicket. Our neighbors were not the nosy kind. Anyway, we had bushes for privacy. In these parts there are no homeowners' associations or restrictive covenants to prevent this kind of thing.

We were pragmatic and resourceful. We were not constipated. We always neatly buried our deposits. We were not savages, after all.

This all came about after my wife and I had lived in an old house out in the county for about five years. The toilet flushed well enough, most of the time, except when our relatives visited. Then the thing flushed slowly, reluctantly. After the relatives had gone I would scrub the tank valve, then run coathangers and Drano through the tiny outlets under the lip of the bowl. All wasted effort, of course. I was avoiding the reekingly obvious, drifting deep in the fetid currents of denial.

An inevitable morning came, late in winter, when the device again got sluggish in response to my own ablutions. And I noticed something unusual in the backyard, just outside the bathroom window, before heading to my office. A puddle. I drove off trying not to dwell on it. The next morning I took a shovel and poked at a patch of sod that was now under an inch of water. I scraped away mud to expose big chunks of slimy wood that seemed to be... floating... until I punched through into deeper water. I stopped, found a long willow branch, and probed the dark abyss.

Time to call in a professional, I thought. February. Mud wherever the ground was not frozen, fresh snow expected tonight.

It was twilight by the time Alman, a dirtwork man I knew, arrived pulling a backhoe on a trailer behind his dual-axle pickup. By now his day should have been over, a strenuous one no doubt. Instead he unloaded and started the machine with its bar of floodlights, gently pushed down and rolled over my flimsy fence, jockeyed around into position and got down to the job itself, just as it began to snow.

The snowflakes were bright in the floodlights while he tore into the backyard and, in minutes, reduced it to a swamp of muck and water. He dragged pieces of sodden black railroad ties up from a hiding place six inches below the surface of our lawn. Because our yard through the years had always been unaccountably green, I gradually had taken to believing that Nature favors the neglectful. I may not have been entirely wrong, but wrong enough.

Alman finally dragged away a dozen old timbers that had been covering a cinderblock tank. The hold underneath was splashing full, a sparkling void against the thin snow surrounding it. It was long past twilight by the time he drove his backhoe back up onto its trailer. I put some cash in Alman's left hand and shook his right one. His hard, cold work had left us surrounded by a chewed-up ruin of backhoe tracks, tangled fence wire, mud, and of course, the railroad ties.

Railroad ties are saturated with creosote. They are thick, heavy, and long-lasting, but they rot eventually when immersed. My ties probably came from the Dolores & Rio

Grande or the McPhee Railroad of a century ago when trains ran all through these valleys and forests. The narrow-gauge trains carried timber, machinery, and fruit. Spur lines collected timber destined for a Denver box factory. This is fine fruit country and the foothills were covered in orchards once— apples, peaches, cherries, apricots, even one foolhardy stand of avocados. Everything you need to stay regular.

***

The next professional who visited us came a few days later, in a special truck driven at some expense from a town fifty miles away. It was a tanker truck with a cute company name and cute logo, and it came equipped with a large pump and a fat hose. The driver was a jolly-looking man with a broad moustache and strong, hairy arms. He wore bright orange coveralls and black rubber gloves. He brandished a large hammer with an orange handle.

"Pardner," he said to me in a fatherly (yet not necessarily a clean or healthy) way, "you and I are going to have The Talk. We are going to discuss Poop 101." He grinned with obvious relish. Here was a man who actually knew some shit, and knew that he knew it, and was professionally empowered to spread it around.

I don't remember profound or novel insights enlivening the jolly man's well-polished Talk, but he delivered critical knowledge for which I was long overdue, facts of life neglected by my parents and teachers: Poop, once fallen into a septic tank, dissolves (mostly) and the sludge flows laterally through an array of perforated pipes—known as a *leech field* in waste management circles, the name recalling macabre medieval medical procedures. The excremental fluid seeps out of the pipes then magically disappears into the earth. When the magic doesn't happen fast enough, a big pumper truck with a cute logo extends a thick hose behind the flowers through the metallic throat of your tank, sucks your troubles away, then drives off.

None of this prim story applied to the situation in my back yard. What I had was a cinderblock pond, brimful with liquid shit, currently surrounded by a mud bog. Somewhere out beyond Ground Zero lay the inert remnants of a leech field long dry, its frail pipes clogged with clay or choked with a spidery rootwork from summers long dead and gone.

This cinderblock tank, now open to the sky, had been our septic system entire. Whatever comfort we had enjoyed through the years happened thanks to porous cinderblock, stacked without mortar, the rich effluent slowly percolating through the backyard—a simple and altogether natural process, in fact a near-perfect exoneration of the Neglect principle, at least until the roof fell in.

Getting the big pumper truck into position was a bit awkward, its hose barely reaching into the dark pond. We lost the poppy patch and some trim on the tool shed. The orange-suited man used his orange-handled hammer to pound a few snaps and seals on the hose end, then switched on his pump. It ran for about four minutes while the surface of the dark fluid receded. Then the pump shuddered and went abruptly silent.

"I'm done," he said, giving me his pity grin. You poor sucker. "Too much debris down there. Debris clogs the hose, burns out the pump. Not worth it."

Not worth it, I thought. *No, not worth it even for the standard house-call, not to mention the surcharge for mileage, the poppies, and the shed....*

Then the jolly man and pumper truck were gone. I stood alone, staring at a chaos of contamination, nonsensical shapes poking up through the glistening coal-sheen surface, musing: *what a complete load of crap.*

I knew what I had to do.

On a shelf in the shed I had a disposable coverall, given me by a friend who worked as a hospital operating room technician. It was a white zip-up, complete with feet, hood, and gloves. The shed also contained a pair of tall rubber boots, a ladder, rake, shovel, and tin bucket.

The rest of the day was routine: climb down the ladder to the slick submerged floor of the chamber, scoop or rake or somehow maneuver stuff into the bucket (depending on the shape and consistency of particular pieces), climb the ladder with bucket in hand, step out to cross the mud apron, walk randomly to some new spot in the snowy field, and pour fragrant muck upon the earth. Return empty, descend the ladder, fill the bucket, and so forth.

Deep in the tank I found and cut taproots from nearby trees and pelagic mats of rootlets. Some things were harder to explain. A wrench. A scythe. Some kind of wheel. Sections of iron pipe. Pieces of a plastic picture frame. Bits and pieces I carried up the ladder and set aside, returning with the shovel to fill the bucket again with smooth, dark gravy and dumplings.

***

I might have mentioned the fragrance, but in fact I don't recall much smell at all, at least not after getting started. Imagine a massive old tree falling in the forest, and landing smack across your nose—would there be a smell?

You might wonder why I went on doing this, gradually emptying the pit, knowing in my guts that an entirely new tank was the only plausible remedy. I have asked this question myself. The answer might be, *Now I know for sure I have been baptized. Bathed in the blood of the lamb, as it were. Initiated into fundamental truths about the carbon cycle, about peristalsis and metabolism. Face to face with the Medusa.*

Big deal, I'm thinking now. It was merely a baptism, a first taste. Less pleasant work is always necessary. Some people, a hereditary caste of Kolkata sewer cleaners for instance, bathe in the stuff daily, and I've heard the corpse business is grimmer still. As humanity is dispensable, so humility is indispensable. But even so.

Another answer: we really did want a sewer of some kind to get us and ours through until the spring. We wanted an indoor commode and an occasional shower. And from a certain point of view, the system was now at least halfway fixed: the toilet did flush more freely, since it poured out of a blackish pipe and through the fresh air into a pool at the bottom of the pit right outside the bedroom window.

Over the next few days we spanned the pit with two-byfours. We found tin sheets to fit over these, weighted them down with a few rocks to secure them from the coming windstorms, and carried on. Fortunately it was the backyard and not facing the road. Anyway, the county real estate market has stunk in recent years, especially in late winter.

Some weeks later, Alman returned with his backhoe to smooth down the last of the debris. He tumbled the cinderblock monstrosity down into its own hollow and buried it in a hash of old clay and a dump truck's worth of fill soil. As Alman moved the earth around he turned up a big orange-handled hammer. I keep it for an amulet.

Eventually, in the spring when our thin pasture was dappled with patches of thick green growth, a third kind of professional arrived on the scene. Burly men in hardhats installed a solid cement tank and buried long rows of new, roomy infiltrators. It was a massive and modern system. Now our metabolic byproducts are whisked away in the modern manner, out of sight, out of mind.

EVERYTHING IN ITS RIGHT PLACE

Eric Scot Tryon

THE YEAR WAS 1997. My best friend Jeremy and I were sophomores at UC Santa Barbara (Go Gauchos!). It was Friday night, and we were heading out of the booze-flooded, short skirt-infested town of Isla Vista and into Santa Barbara to see some music (Buck-O-Nine to be exact—late nineties ska was all the rage). Jeremy opted to drive as he had a company van, but since it was our first time at the venue, we weren't entirely sure how to get there. And for the record, Jeremy was feeling just fine when we left.

But as we exited what we thought was the correct exit, Jeremy announced, "Ooh, man, I gotta take a wicked shit." Now, a 19-year-old male announcing a bowel movement is as commonplace as "what's up?" or "check ya later." I thought nothing of it.

A couple left turns, right turns, and U-turns later, he reiterated with emphasis. "Oh man, this shit's a-comin'!"

Okay, okay, I thought, maybe I should take a little more interest in helping him find this place. But somehow we ended up more near the beach than downtown. We're not even close, I realized. But, of course, I couldn't share this with Jeremy. He was already white-knuckling the steering wheel as it was, and I think he even levitated an inch or two off his seat in order to keep everything in its right place.

"Dude, I'm not going to make it!" he squealed. "I gotta find a shitter!"

I knew he meant business. But even now, in a simple search for a public restroom, his turns weren't making any sense. He was, as they say, no longer fit to operate heavy machinery. It was his ass that was piloting the vehicle, trying to follow its shit-compass.

And then, just when I thought he was going to have an accident of Hindenburg magnitude, as Jeremy was rising higher and higher above the driver's seat, he spotted a restroom.

"Shit!" he yelled as he jerked the steering wheel to the right and pulled up alongside the curb. We were at a park near the beach, and there, like a beacon of gastrointestinal salvation, stood a Spanish-style public restroom. It looked clean and well kept, with its beige stucco and rust-colored ceramic tile roof. Jeremy threw the car into park and flew out the door in a panicked blur.

(Granted, this is technically where I leave the story to innocently sit in the van, wait for Jeremy, and ponder where the hell the venue was. But for the sake of the dramatic, I will tell it as if I was right there with him the whole while, maybe even letting him squeeze my hand.)

Legs reaching, arms pumping, Jeremy raced like a world-class sprinter around the backside of the small building to find the door with the blue sign sporting an "M" and a little stick-man savior. Jeremy's frenzied fingers wrapped around the metal handle. He yanked with a frenetic strength, telling his body to please, just squeeze for a moment longer!

Locked.

Let's pause for a moment shall we (since we as readers have this luxury, something mind you, that Jeremy did not). Even with all the students, hippies and yuppies, Santa Barbara thrives off having everything in its right place and appearing to be oh so prim and proper. This means spending millions in sidewalk art along State Street, and this means ignoring the homeless but making sure stores have a dog bowl outside for Princess and Tinkerbell. And, in Jeremy's case, this also means all public restrooms will be locked precisely at sundown. But try explaining all this to an about to detonate colon.

As soon as Jeremy had left the van, he crossed the point of no return. The visual confirmation of a restroom sprung his body into action. He was mobilizing the troops. There was no turning back.

"I had no choice," Jeremy later told me, in a tone so somber you thought he might have killed a man. And so there, on the cement walkway, just mere yards from the bathroom, Jeremy dropped his pants. The sigh of relief could be heard from Santa Maria to Oxnard.

The danger, however, was only momentarily averted. As we all know, the urgency of a bowel movement is often directly proportional to the looseness of its consistency. Jeremy soon found himself spraying out a mini Lake Superior right there on the cement. And the dance to avoid "getting his feet wet" could make the best of river dancers envious. (This is the part of the story Jeremy usually acts out for his audience: legs spread wide, dancing and shuffling about on the tips of his toes. He turns out to be quite agile for a stocky guy.)

Thanks to his fancy footwork, his shoes were spared, and safely back in the van, the story was told to me in excessive detail. Luckily, this wasn't Jeremy's first rodeo. In pure survival mode, he had instinctively grabbed a handful of Kleenex on his way out of the van. We did make it to the show in time, and I was only asked to smell Jeremy's pinky once.

As a fitting epilogue, Jeremy's dad came to visit several weeks later. And during a relaxing walk along the beach on a gorgeous Santa Barbara afternoon, Jeremy and his father passed by the infamous bathroom. Jeremy pointed to the cement and showed his pops the faded but very present remnants of that night—like the chalk outline of a slain Great Lake.

"My dad couldn't have been more proud," Jeremy still recounts.

A COUP ON THE GOD OF DECENCY

John Fox

MR. BARBER, MY HISTORY TEACHER in high school, said that in his marriage, they had far too much respect for one another to watch each other defecate. He drew out the three syllables of the word defecate, as if to emphasize its dirtiness. In comparison, "shit" sounded clean. Of course we asked about peeing. "You mean urinating?" he said, glowering over us and our foul mouths. His glowering was more intimidating than Mrs. Snively's glowering, because as the high school football coach Mr. Barber weighed in at 300 lbs and bench-pressed 475 back in his professional body building days. He still had a chest that appeared to be hiding genetically modified pumpkins. Apparently, as Mr. Barber taught us in our sophomore year, defecating and urinating both belonged to same category: the ultra-private, the never-to-be-mentioned, much less to be seen. Not even in the most intimate of relationships—a husband and wife—could a husband witness fluid or solid matter pass from his wife.

None of us could believe that he and Mrs. Barber were able to maintain such fanatical divisions of bathroom time. We devised increasingly elaborate scenarios of "What if...?" Mr. Barber insisted that if he had to brush his teeth, he would wait until his wife was finished. Mr. Barber insisted that if he had to pee so badly it might back up his urinary tract and give him an infection, he would go in his backyard rather than barge in on her [Mental note: only teepee front yard]. Mr. Barber insisted that if he were on a desert island with his wife, she would duck behind a coconut tree. Mr. Barber insisted that if the entire desert island was a two-foot strip of sand, and if the coconut tree was not wide enough to block his wife's urination, and if he could not turn around since his legs and back were broken, he would close his eyes and hum to himself until she gave the all-clear. We could not break the man.

"Can we go to the bathroom?" we asked.

"Are you going to take a bath?" he said.

"Can we go to the restroom?" we asked. And then he would relent and hand us the ruler hall pass. No one ever asked him whether that meant we were going to take a rest in the restroom. A former professional bodybuilder has a way of squelching freedom of speech. Naturally, this prudish behavior about passing waste made us wonder about sex. Because we did not know much about sex but believed we knew everything, and more importantly, acted in front of others as if we knew everything, our questions were relatively innocent. Did they sleep in the same beds? They did. Did they have sex with a sheet with a hole in it? They did not. What about farting in front of his wife? "You mean passing gas?" he said, glowering. We relented. Passing gas, yes. "I have never willingly passed gas in front of my wife. In the rare times when I do, I always excuse myself." Since we didn't want to think too much about Mr. Barber and his wife having sex, we focused on the farting taboo, which was crazy enough.

I have no idea when we actually studied history that year. Half of the class was sex ed, if hearing about Mr. Barber's aversions to bodily functions and his fastidious cleanliness during the act of love-making truly counted as sex ed. I think we made most of our history up. That might explain why for years I believed the Tibetan-Nazi forces defeated the Japanese redcoats at Waterloo during the Revolutionary War. But if we did not learn about history, we did learn about the God of Decency. Mr. Barber never actually spoke that venerable name, but he pounded the laws into us with admirable efficiency.

Breaking laws of proper hygiene and conduct was an affront to God. More importantly, this was also an affront to the God beyond God, the God of Decency. The God of Decency was a tribal god of fierce loyalties, strange sacrifices and inscrutable rules. His ten commandants decreed the proper decencies to all ages and all peoples, and woe to those heathens who dared not cover their mouth with an elbow during a sneeze, and woe to those who used improper words like "butt" or "ass" or even, God-forbid, "shit," and woe to those Sodomites and Gomorrahites whose husbands did not avert their face when their wives popped a squat.

***

I should come clean right now and confess I have not abided by the commandments of the God of Decency. Oh, far from it. I have wallowed in many a pigsty, in much defecation. I have displayed myself on every high hill, under every spreading tree. I have sinned against Italian walls by pissing on their stucco and have pictures taken by my traveling companions to prove it. I have stained Greek ruins in front of tour groups and I have golden-showered wooden fence-posts in northern Argentina. I have even, in front of passing schoolchildren, baptized Cambodian foliage in yellow from the second story of a colonial mansion.

More than that, I have not shielded myself from my wife, nor my wife from me. I have seen her piss, poop, and vomit. She has seen me piss, poop, and vomit. Sometimes, in cases of food poisoning, altitude/car sickness, or pressurized bladders, we have simultaneously pissed, pooped and/or vomited. We do it on the train, we do it in the rain. What's more, we have both smelled each other's farts. We have both tried to make each other smell our farts. We have cupped our anuses and caught some air and smothered each other's noses, and we have covered-wagoned each other and we have bent over while the other was sleeping and released it straight into their face.

Caveat: perhaps some things were only done by me.

But even beyond mere witnessing, I have recorded such acts. In the dire circumstance of needing to pee but being hours and miles away from restrooms, my wife yanked down her Smurf-colored REI pants and let loose on top of lava rocks. This was recorded for posterity by my Nokia point-and-shoot. I was not embarrassed. I was gleeful. I was laughing. In some corner of our hard drives, there are several pictures of us in various stages of undress, sometimes holding a hand out toward the camera as if to block it, sometimes laughing in amazement, sometimes hamming it up for the lens. This has not been an isolated occurrence. It has happened across borders and across years. Most of the time the cameras in question belonged to us.

But hear me out, oh ye haters and judgers out there, ye enforcers and mercenaries and devotees of the God of Decency. I have the best excuse in the world. I am a traveler. Travelers have no pot to call their own, no private door behind which to do their dirty work. Instead, we have to forge out into the wild blue yonder and release our bowels where we may. We are forced into such primitive situations, we do not seek them out. Okay, we seek them out a little. For the story. For the picture. But the point is, sometimes it might be necessary to break a few of the laws of modesty regarding emission of bodily fluids/solids.

In utter humility, here is my ultimate defense for breaking down the commandments of the God of Decency: Health. That's right, staying healthy. Because when you're on the road, far from your HMO and PPO and Kaiser and All-Purpose Blankie-Charm, who might you consult about your health? Ding Ding Ding! That's right, your feces. Your feces are a prime indicator for how your bowels are working. And if you're eating food from carts in third world countries or making the tremendous mistake of cooking raw calamari in a vat of boiling oil in Vietnam, or eating dubious hamburgers from the square in Bolivia served by an unshaven man who has probably never washed his hands, you will need more than a little information, trust me.

Do you know what your feces are telling you? Perhaps you should call in a referee, an impartial judge, a kind of medium that can communicate with poop how others call up the dead. They will read your poop like tea leaves. They will look deep into your bowels and divine your future. You are too compromised. The poop comes from your own body, so you naturally will misread it. Here is where the significant other comes in. They are your Poop Reader. When you have squatted over a toilet bowl with no seat and no water and released several volleys of feces that have felt out of the normal run of things, call in your Poop Reader to discern the faint signs inside that toilet bowl. It works even better if the Poop Reader is present during the process, because then the Poop Reader can discern even more information from the length, the strain, the sounds.

Over many years, working together, my wife and I developed a taxonomy of poops. This taxonomy is like a secret books of kells, or secret Kabbalah information—known only to initiates, highly secretive, and hard to come by—so treasure it well. Although this is certainly heresy to the God of Decency, I offer it in the spirit of health and under the Freedom Of Feces Act (FOFA).

Soft Serve: Otherwise known as lava. Also known as Slurpee. This comes out like a frosty freeze at icecreamville. If you swirl your butt, you can pile it up in a conical shape. Your body was unable to process something. Switch food sources.

Kibbles and Bits: Looks like eponymous dog food. Or, if you're into other animals, larger than hamster droppings and smaller than camel droppings. Same shape though. Sometimes clumped together. Also known as Cocoa Pebbles. Means you're not getting enough fiber in your diet. Ditch the processed food and eat some veggies.

Shotgun: Splatters the bowl like a double-barrel would splatter brains. Messy all over. Makes the hostel workers hate you. You got some bad juju in the water or food. Swallow some Ciprofloxacin or get thyself to a doctor pronto.

Log Rider: Yeah, like the ride at Disneyland. A massive turd, able to hold multiple individuals, it dwarfs the toilet bowl itself. Often a sign of the end of constipation, because you've been saving up. Work on being more regular.

Technicolored Dream Poop: In the normal brown of the feces, wedges of color appear. Often green, sometimes red. Sometimes you have the extremely rare combination of both green and red, known as a Technicolored Christmas Poop. This variant of poop is not harmful or painful and provides no health worries.

Moby Dick: A variant of the technicolored dream poop, and worthy of its own category because of its rarity. Pasty or ghostly white. Not straight-up albino, just a haze of white. No idea what makes this action. But take a picture for posterity or you'll go all Ahab chasing it down a second time.

Peanut Brittle: Feels like a stiff wedge of the famous candy pressing itself out your ass. Painful as hell. Eat some fruit and it'll soften up.

Jalapeño Poopers: Spicy! Hot Damn! Cut down on the hot sauce, amigo. Your cornhole can't handle the fire.

***

I have seen the children's books like *Everyone Poops* and *Once Upon A Potty* and they don't go far enough. We need a masterpiece that will last through all generations, and I am here with a brilliant suggestion: *What Does Your Poop Say?* On the front cover, an animated turd. It will have eyes. It won't be too bumpy or scaly, more like the ideal Platonic version of poop. It will be roughly seven inches long, mas o menos, accounting for animated distortions. At the end, it will have a mouth like a snake, as though someone has made a cut and wedged it open. A dialogue bubble will come from the poop's mouth. It will say something intelligent, like "Buy this book now!" or "You have long worms in your small colon," or "Stop eating so much Salsa!" This book will sell millions. No, billions, accounting for translation rights and several generations. This book will work like Nietzsche upon the God of Decency. False beliefs will be stripped away. Former idols will be cast down. A new age of Aquarius will dawn, where every citizen will enjoy the freedom of shitting and pissing in the new excrement-friendly city of the future.

THE POOPY DRUMMER

Bob Jere

I THINK EVERYONE reading this would agree that there is never a good time to have diarrhea, especially at a concert, and it's worse if you're the one playing the concert. There is an old saying in show business, "The show must go on." I'm here to tell you, whoever said that was not a drummer who had the runs!

I play drums for a popular band based out of Orange County, California (whose name I'll leave out for obvious reasons). We travel nationwide on a regular basis. A few years ago, on Labor Day weekend, we were doing a string of three concerts in the Los Angeles area. This was nice because we are usually on the road that time of year. On my way home from Saturday's show I thought I would stop and get something to eat. There was a sandwich shop on the way home (I won't mention their name, but it has to do with an underground train system). They closed at 10 p.m. and I squeaked in at 9:58. The manager said, "Hey, we're closed!" He looked to be about eighteen, had greasy hair, bad acne, a mouth full of metal, and a bad attitude. You know the guy.

"Come on, bro, it's 9:58. I have two minutes and I'm starving! Can you please give me a break?"

He looked at me disgusted, shrugged his shoulders and said, "Cha... whatever... what-do-ya want, dude?"

"Thank you!" I replied, "I'll take a foot-long meatball please."

He made me my sandwich and I was on my way. Once again, all was right with the world. I won the manager over and got my sandwich, I was on the way home to my house, not some smelly hotel room, and I was going to spend the rest of the evening with my wife—life was good. When I got home I was greeted at the door by my dog. As usual, she was very excited to see me, but even more so on this night. She could smell the food! She knows I'm a sucker for her and will give her a bite or two of whatever I'm eating.

I changed and got comfortable, opened a cold beer, and turned the TV to *Saturday Night Live*. My wife came and sat with me and our dog. It was time to enjoy my sandwich! I unwrapped it and the smell of marinara sauce and meatballs filled the room.

"Mmm, that smalls good," said my wife.

I offered her half, but she had already eaten, and declined. My dog on the other hand, sat staring, begging for the first bite, but that was to be savored by me, the master! The moment had arrived, my first bite. I put the sandwich to my mouth, took a bite and... *That's a little weird*. It didn't taste like the meatball sandwich I had come to know and love. Not bad, just not the same... *Oh well*, chomp, chomp, chomp. I gave a bite to my dog. BOOM!! Gone, down the hatch! I gave her another bite. BAM! Gone! Faster than the first bite.

"I wish you wouldn't feed her like that," said my wife.

"I know. Sorry."

I finished my sandwich, and we finished watching *Saturday Night Live*. It had one of the funniest skits I'd ever seen on *S.N.L.* entitled "Roy Rules." My wife and I laughed until we cried. After that we were both tired, and I had a gig the next day, so off to bed we went. About 3:30 a.m. I was awakened by the sound of panting, bad dog breath, and my dog staring me in the face.

"She has to go out now," my wife said. "I told you not to feed her that late."

"Damn it," I said, getting up to let my dog out. She hopped and sprinted to the side door in the kitchen. I opened the door and she bolted to the grass. SPPLLLLLLLAAAAAT!! *Wow! Her stomach is really messed up.* I walked into the dark yard to make sure she was ok. She was still across the yard from me and I could hear her stomach turning. Gggggrrrrrrrruuuuuup! Gggggggrrrrrruuuuuuuup. *The poor thing.* Again, Gggggrrrrrrrrrup, Gggggggrrrrrrrrrrrrrup. *Man, not only could I hear that, I think I felt it too... wait... that's not her stomach, it's mine. SHIT!!!!* I sprinted back into the house, made it to the bathroom with no time to spare. SPLLLLLLLLLAAAAAAAT!!!!!! At that point I realized I had poisoned both myself and my dog.

"Is everything ok?" I heard from the bedroom.

"Yeah, babe, everything's fine."

I didn't want my wife to know I had made both the dog and myself sick. She hates it when I feed the dog from the table and I didn't want or need to hear about it at this point. Again SPLLLLLLLLLLLLLLLLLAAAAAAAAAAAAAAT! *Man, you had to eat the whole thing,* I chastised myself. *You couldn't stop at half? That will teach you to be such glutton.*

I cleaned up, got my dog from outside, and back to bed I went.

Ten minutes later, she was in the yard again and I was back in the restroom. When I was finished I washed my hands, opened the door and there she was, my wife, staring at me with her arms folded. "You fed the dog some of your sandwich, from the table, and now both of you are sick, aren't you?"

"Yep," I replied.

"The poor dog."

"Hey, what about me?"

I went into the kitchen, brought my dog back in, got some Pepto and went back to bed. POW!!!!! ZOOOM!!!!! I'm back in the bathroom and my dog was outside once again. *That was some kind of bad sandwich! I've shit out way more than a foot-long's worth, that's for sure.* This went on the rest of the night. Up and down, in and out of bed.

Around 9 a.m., the dog was fine, sleeping in her bed, but I was still at it. Every five minutes, SPPPPLLLLLLAAAAAAT. *How can one human body hold that much fluid? Were the hell is all of this coming from?*

About this time I was starting to get worried. We had a big show that night, opening for southern rock legends, The Outlaws. The show was at a very nice concert venue in Long Beach. It would be our first time playing there, and the show was sold out. We had to play great. I sent my wife to the store to get more Pepto, Mylanta, Pepcid AC, Tums, anything she could get her hands on to make this evil shit sandwich I had eaten go the hell away.

She came home and I started dosing myself with the over the counter medicine. It felt and tasted like I was eating chalk. Nothing helped. *I know, I'll have a cheese sandwich. That'll plug me up.* Nothing! Still every fifteen minutes... SPPPPLLLLAAAT! This went on all day until I had to leave for load-in and sound-check.

I got to the gig and the guys knew something was up. The bass player looked at me and asked, "Been up all night?"

"Yes."

"DUDE!! This is a big gig for us! Why the hell would you stay up all night partying when you knew that?!"

"No, bro, it's not like that at all." As I was explaining what had happened, Grrrrrrrruuuuuuuuup, Grrrrrrrruuuuuuuuuuup. "FUCK!! Where's the bathroom?!" I screamed as I bolted toward the restroom. I ran into a large brick restroom with metal stalls. As the door flew open it smashed into the wall and then slammed shut behind me, making a sound like a prison cell door. BOOM! I noticed the guitar player standing at a urinal taking a piss, but I didn't have time for pleasantries. I slammed the metal stall door shut and SPPPPLLLLAAAAAAT! The echo was deafening! From the other side of the metal divider I heard, "You okay, bro? OH MY GOD!! COUGH GAG, GAG COUGH!" I heard the restroom door open and slam closed, then I heard the laughter all the way down the hall for the next five minutes.

After cleaning up, I went into the dressing room to find my band—my friends, my brothers in arms—laughing their asses off.

"Fuck you, guys. This is not funny."

"No, it's pretty funny, bro!" said the guitar player with an evil, cackling laugh.

"Have you tried Pepcid AC? That always works for me," suggested the bass player.

"Dude, I've taken everything."

"Here, just take some more—you need to do something," he said, handing me the box he kept in his guitar case. "I never leave home without it. You never know when something like this is going to happen. Just keep the box."

Somehow, sound-check went pretty well. Afterward, I ordered another cheese sandwich, and then proceeded to eat the entire box of Pepcid AC for dessert. Still, every ten minutes I would make a mad dash for the restroom, holding my ass cheeks together with both hands, fly through the door, round the corner, shut the stall just in the nick of time for SPPPPPLLLLLLAAAAAT! *How does the human body hold this much shit? It's not like I'm a fat ass or something.* Every time, I returned to the dressing room to the sound of laughter from my friends.

"I'm glad you guys find this so funny."

"Oh, we do, bro, we do," one of them said.

"Why don't you just cork it up with a broken drum stick, dude?"

"Good idea... dick."

"FIVE MINUTES!" The stage manager yelled into the room. *Shit, this is going to suck so bad,* I thought to myself as I ran to the restroom one last time. The good news here was we were the opening act, not the headliner. That meant we only had to play for forty-five minutes, not an hour and a half with an encore. The bad news was, of course, I was the drummer! I use both legs in a pumping motion, all night, nonstop, and I had water shooting out of my ass like a fire hose!

We were behind the curtain, everyone was in place, I was

behind my drums, and everything felt pretty good. They turned the house lights off and the crowd started to roar. I counted in the first song as the curtain was opening and just tried to go into auto pilot mode. We finished the first two songs and I felt ok. The crowd was diggin' it. As I started the third song, I felt the familiar rumble, Grrrrrrrrrrrruuuuuuuuuup. *No. Not Now!* I focused on the music. *Hey, it subsided a little… wait, no it didn't!* Grrrrrrrrrrrrrrrruuuuuuuuuuuuuuuuuuuuuuuuup. *Oh my God, not now!* All I could do was grit my teeth and play.

If I scoot from side to side a little, and squish my butt cheeks together, that will help, and it did for a minute or two. *Just don't think about it and keep smiling. No one will know.* Grrrrrrrruuuuuuuuuuuuuup. *OHHHHH MAN! That one felt like it moved from the bottom of my diaphragm all the way down to my butt-hole.* Now I was in pain. *Maybe if I fart that will relieve some of the pressure,* I thought for a second. *NO!!! That would be the stupidest gamble in the history of stupid gambles, you idiot! There is no way I am going to shit my pants on stage…* Grrrrrrrrrrrrrrrrrrruuuuuuuuuuuuuuuuuuuuuuuup! *Or am I?*

Thank God, only one song left, I thought as I looked at the set list. *It's a long tune, with a lot of double bass, but you can hold it together, champ,* I thought, trying to give myself a boost of confidence. The song seemed to go on forever, while my stomach went Grrrrrrrrrrrruuup, Grrrrrrrrrrruuuuup, again and again. *Scoot side to side again, pinch your butt cheeks, Big Guy. Almost there…almost there.* Boom!! We got to the end of the song, hit the final chord and the show was over. I did it! I made it through the longest forty-five minutes of my life and I didn't shit myself! I was proud, prouder maybe than someone my age should have been for successfully not shitting their pants, really just damn happy I was not the laughing stock of the Southern California music scene.

You still have to exit the stage, dude. Don't get cocky. The demon in my stomach was about to explode and shoot out my asshole, but I walked to the front of the stage and took a bow with the band. The sound from the crowd was deafening. *Please, God, don't let them ask for an encore,* I thought for the first time in my life.

"ONE MORE, ONE MORE!!" the crowd chanted as I slowly walked to the side of the stage. SNAP, the house lights came on.

"No encore from the openers," the stage manager grumbled. *Thank God!*

"Take care of my drums!!" I yelled to our road manager as I sprinted backstage. I flew down two flights of stairs, rounded the corner, sprinted down the hall, up a ramp, and slammed the door, open—BOOM!!—flew into the stall, tore my pants down, and.......pppppt. *That's it? A fart? That couldn't have happened three hours ago? Hell, that couldn't have happened forty-eight minutes ago?*

I would have been mad if I hadn't been so happy it was over.

Now, I know a lot of you who are reading this are probably thinking, "It would have been funnier if he would have shit his pants." Well maybe for everyone except me. Hell, after taking all the meds and eating four or five cheese sandwiches, I couldn't shit at all for about five days. So without a big dramatic ending of crapping my pants, why did I share this story at all? Well, I thought it might make you think. Next time you go to a concert, really look at the faces the drummer makes while he or she is playing and think to yourself, "What's really going on up there?"

COLOSTOMY CALVIN

Daniel A. Roberts

THERE WASN'T A SOUL on the planet who could have prepared me for the experiences that awaited me as a Certified Nursing Assistant. One of those more notable experiences was my time with an old World War II veteran the staff at one nursing home nicknamed Colostomy Calvin.

If you don't know what a colostomy is, be glad. Usually those who do know are the ones who either care for colostomy patients, or have one installed themselves. In layman's terms, the lower abdomen has a hole opened up and the large intestine is cut and pulled through the side. It's stitched in place and a device called a colostomy appliance is placed over it. That's for the bag to be attached, where the feces, or I should say shit, is collected.

Colostomy bags are easily attached and removed. Back in the mid 1990's, they were also paper thin. That coupled with an old man who survived World War II and suffered a touch of senility, well, all hell would break loose on a daily basis. My first encounter with this wicked combination was during my first day on the job. Certified Nursing Assistants clean asses on a regular basis, so poop normally doesn't bother us. The poor Registered Nurses who never worked as a CNA, however, became the regular target of Colostomy Calvin's twisted ire.

Vickie was an attractive young blonde fresh out of college. She worked as a Registered Nurse on the same floor I did and was hired the day before me. This wasn't unusual—nursing homes in Florida tend to have a high turnover rate. As the shift started, Colostomy Calvin's thunderous voice blasted out of his doorway: "Die, ya fucking Kraut, die!"

With those words echoing down the hall, a full colostomy bag hit Vicki in the head as she passed his doorway.

Please understand, it wasn't pretty. Ever been hit by a water balloon? That's the effect, only this wasn't water. It was half-formed shit with the consistency of warm jello. Vickie's scream would have curdled the blood of a demon. Half of her head got plastered with dripping shit, flowing like mud all down her side and front. Her traumatized reaction wasn't unwarranted.

I dropped all but two of the fresh towels I'd been carrying and threw one over Vickie's head while pressing the other in her hands. She understood immediately and began toweling the smelly mess off. I turned and got my first ever visual of this man.

He was sitting in his wheelchair, his shirt pulled up, and resting on the upper bulge of his belly, the colostomy appliance missing its bag. He was laughing!

"Why did you do that?" I heard myself asking in complete shock. If I had been working there longer and knew the rest of the staff and their history better, I could have saved myself the time. But my buzzing brain had to know right then, directly from the guilty shooter.

"No steak," he rasped. "No wine. No goddamned cake for my birthday. Those Krauts give me nothing but shit, so I give it right back!"

I tried in vain not to chuckle, as his response caught me off guard. He was quite serious in his reasoning, which made it a little funnier than it should have been. I left the room before he could elaborate and found Vickie was already gone to use one of the many in-house shower stalls.

Colostomy Calvin was far from done. He was out of ammo

for the rest of the shift, but there was already new ammo on its way.

***

Calvin's yell for help came during my second day, only hours into the shift. "I slipped, somebody help me! Damn it, I broke my fucking hip!"

I braced to run into his room but Mindy, who had worked there as a CNA for more than three years, grabbed my arm. "Don't," she warned me. "It's a trap." The reasoning was sound. I quickly remembered that Colostomy Calvin was wheelchair-bound and couldn't walk. My natural reaction to a cry for help merely kicked in, but Mindy saved me from a shitty fate.

Vickie, on the other hand, wasn't fortunate enough to have any staff nearby to stop her from charging into his room. She was a brand new Registered Nurse after all, and even though she earned a bag of trauma laced shit the previous day, her caring spirit took over and she rushed in to help.

Thwack!

She came reeling out backwards, a shattered colostomy bag falling from her forehead, jello-like shit dripping all down her face and front. Colostomy Calvin's derision followed her out of the room. "Got ya again, you fucking Kraut! Ha!"

Vickie resigned from the nursing home that day and I learned she wasn't the only staff member Calvin had gloriously driven off with his shit-loaded grenades. The current score was Colostomy Calvin: 12; Nursing Home Staff: 0. If you ever wondered why there was a high turnover among the new staff, I think you're figuring out the answer to that little mystery!

Colostomy Calvin was on my shower list on that second morning, and I was determined to talk to this dangerous shit shooter as the hot water was raining down on him. I discussed the situation with no small amount of disgruntled wonder.

"You made Vickie quit," I informed the old man while his twisted smile got wider. "She was only here to help you. Do you understand that?"

"She's not the first Kraut I killed, she won't be the last

48

either. Fucking Hitler can't stop sending them my way, so I give them all the shit I can unleash!" His twisted chuckle made my blood turn cold. "When I get my steak and wine and my goddamned birthday cake, the war is over, hear me?"

I could almost hear the choir of angels in the background. Could this be the answer to his senile mind? Maybe a steak dinner, some wine, and a piece of cake would stop his shit attacks on the staff.

After my shift ended, I found myself knocking on the door for the Director of Nurses. "Come in," an older women in a business suit greeted me. I told her of my conversation with Colostomy Calvin and she listened patiently. "No, it's not that," she politely informed me when I was done. "He gets his steak, non-alcoholic wine, and sugar-free cake once a year for his birthday. I wish we could transfer him to another facility, but nobody wants him. For now, we're all he has."

Day three on the job arrived with trepidation.

I visited Colostomy Calvin mere minutes after I clocked in, flapping an empty white pillowcase in his doorway. I didn't want to get hit by his shit. "I see it," he rasped. "I respect your white flag, Kraut. Come in and say what you have to say. Any funny business, you're dead."

I timidly stepped into the doorway, ready to dodge and duck out of sight. He sat there in his wheelchair, one eye opened large, the other eye half-closed. His hand rested on the almost full colostomy bag. It was still attached to the appliance. Unbidden, my mind superimposed a World War II uniform on him, the colostomy bag now a grenade that was waiting to be used at a moment's notice.

I reminded him of our conversation in the shower the day before. Without hesitation I dropped the truth on him. "You get your steak, wine, and cake every birthday. Isn't that enough?" Addled mind or not, he knew the difference!

"You call that piece of leather steak? That wine couldn't get a fucking flea drunk and the cake tastes like shit! So I give them shit right back! Give me a real steak, real wine and some fucking American cake that at least pretends to be sweet, you goddamned Kraut!"

As I carefully left, my mind buzzed. No, he couldn't have the real deal, I knew this already. As the day wore on, his doorway became a lonely strip of hallway once again. Then it happened. Calvin called out with his raspy voice: "I slipped and broke my hip, damn it! Help me!"

There I was, on my third day of work and already a battle-hardened member of the staff, ignoring his cry for help. Another half hour went by when something shattered in his room. It was large enough to draw one of the more experienced nurses, Jessica, to peek carefully into his room. "Calvin!" she admonished him. "We're not going to replace that TV! You broke it, now it's gone forever!"

"I don't watch Kraut TV, damn it!" Colostomy Calvin barked back. "You can shove it up your ass! Take all that broken glass back to Hitler and shove it down his goddamned throat!"

Jessica planted her hands on her hips and scolded him as if he was ten years old. "For your information, I'm Irish! And you're in an American nursing home! I have to get housekeeping up here to clean that mess, and I'm making sure you won't have a full colostomy bag either! I'll be back to change that out, Mister. No more shit from you today, you understand me?"

"Yes," Colostomy Calvin replied, meek and humbled!

Was it true? Did Jessica have the magical touch required to actually tame Colostomy Calvin? My mind reeled. The tough old veteran could give some ground after all. His senile mind found a true moment of clarity. Or did it?

Jessica turned carefully, went to walk away, when Calvin's grating voice lashed out, "Guess what?"

Jessica spun on her heal and shouted back, "What now?"

Just as she hollered, the colostomy bag blurred through the doorway and splattered gooey shit all down her face.

"Take that, you fucking Jap!"

***

I was lucky that I never got splattered by Colostomy Calvin

in my five month tenure. When I left for a better paying position at a rival nursing home, Calvin had upped his quit-count to 23 new staff members. In the darker areas of my own mind, I cheered him on. His war for real steak, real wine, and cake that actually tasted sweet might never be won, but the senile old veteran would never give up. I don't know how long Colostomy Calvin survived or how many more shit bombs he plastered all over unsuspecting new hires, but in the end, that old man really gave a shit about his birthday meal. Every. Single. Day.

INDIAN LEG WRESTLING:
A LESSON IN INTIMACY

Holly Vance

CURTIS AND I LAY NAKED in bed, side-by-side. The open window welcomed the moonlight, and the August breeze blew enough to get a tune out of my blinds but not enough to cool us off. It was too hot for sex or sleep, but we were both restless. We took turns filling the room with our drowsy sighs, touching each other lightly with our fingertips, trying to either propel or lull our moods. Suddenly, Curtis propped himself up on his elbow and said, "Hey, you wanna Indian leg wrestle?"

"Do what?"

"It'll be fun."

I had no idea what Indian leg wrestling was, but I did understand the term "wrestling" and groaned internally. I was too hot and too lethargic to find any kind of activity, done naked or no, alluring. Also, rough-housing with my boyfriend seemed completely unromantic to me: I believed that our little wrestling match would somehow lesson my sex appeal, especially since I knew that he would probably win in about ten seconds. I have the athletic ability of an amoeba.

Curtis explained that we would lay with our heads on

opposite ends of the bed and then by using just our legs, try to flip each other over backward—somersault style—off the bed. It sounded ridiculous, but his impetuousness and boyish glee convinced me to give it a try. Peeking over the edge of the bed, I gauged the distance I would probably soon be falling; the bedroom was sparsely furnished, so the only thing I would be cracking my head on was the floor.

I scooted to the other end of the bed and threw my legs in the air. "Now what?" I asked, feeling strangely like a young virgin on her wedding night. Curtis told me to bend my knees, and pressing the soles of his feet to mine, pushed my legs back so that my bum lifted slightly off the mattress. Immediately, I realized that balance would be an issue, so I fanned my arms out for leverage. We finished "warming up" by pushing each other back gently, both of us rocking on our spines. Then, Curtis said that we were to now straighten our legs and apply pressure calf-to-calf. He pushed me back so that I could feel the logistics of the wrestling move: my legs extended perpendicularly, and then the pressure pushing them more parallel over my body, which forced my rear to lift even higher off the mattress.

The match began to heat up, literally and figuratively. He applied a burst of pressure that nearly sent me flipping off the bed, but I gripped the bed sheets and gained momentum as I rocked back into position, throwing my weight forward and rattling his leverage a bit. A jovial, "Whoa!" came from his side of the bed and I found myself giggling. This was kind of fun.

But, as with most men, Curtis took this "match" a little more seriously and wasn't about to let his girlfriend kick his ass at any competitive sport. Curtis sat up onto his elbows, and, leaning forward to add some oomph to his next shove, managed to push my legs back so far that I could have used my kneecaps as sunglasses. This move also raised my ass off the mattress high enough to be level with his face.

I didn't even feel it coming; in fact, when I first heard the sound, I thought it was him.

Nope, it was me.

I ripped the biggest, loudest fart ever. Not a little toot that I could giggle at and say "oops." This fart had bass. And stamina. I was releasing so much gas that I thought my entire body might be deflating. Right in my boyfriend's, my lover's, face. I had visions of his cheeks rippling, his eyes squinting, his dirty-blond hair dancing.

I shot up into a sitting position to catch a glimpse of Curtis flipping backward: arms flung up in the air, legs forming a huge V as he tipped over the side of the bed. He hit the floor with a boom that probably woke up my downstairs neighbor.

Well shit, at least I won. The sheer force of my gas, not the power of my legs, made me the night's champion of Indian leg wrestling.

After releasing a fart that could rival Hurricane Katrina from my naked butt into my boyfriend's face, all I kept thinking was how men don't even want to *acknowledge* that women fart and shit. Hell, when I'm around a man, any man, even those for whom I have no romantic interest for, I feel this undeniable social pressure to pretend that nothing goes in or comes out of my ass. In fact, I might even deny that I have an anus.

Now I was faced with dealing with the aftermath of single-fartedly destroying our sex life. I was horrified and mortified. I cocooned myself in the sheets and faced the opposite direction. Curtis had not made a sound.

Great. I just killed my boyfriend with my ass.

Looking over my shoulder, I saw one of Curtis' hands reach up and grab onto the edge of the bed, then the other one met it. As he hauled himself back up, I quickly turned away again and coiled up. I could hear Curtis panting, could feel the bed shift as he climbed back on.

"Babe, babe," he said breathlessly. He draped himself over my body, trying to see my face, which I was trying desperately to turn away from him.

"I can't look at you," I sputtered between laughs.

"Babe," he repeated. "Look at me."

"I can't!" I gasped. And then, I farted again.

Fart #2 had nothing on fart #1. A minor aftershock. Nevertheless, we both exploded in hysterics.

Once we calmed down—he sprawled on his back, me still cocooned and hiding—I said, "You are going to never want to have sex with me again."

He rolled me over, widened the hole in the sheets so that he could see my entire face. Looking me deep in the eyes, he smiled and touched my face lightly. "Are you kidding," he said, "this is the most intimate experience we've ever had."

WHEAT'S REVENGE

Sarah Marie

UNTIL SHORTLY BEFORE I WAS BORN, Mom and Dad had a large housecat. Wheat, named such because he was muted orange, had personality—of the devilish sort. He was the type of cat who'd intentionally throw litter out of the cat box when it wasn't clean enough to suit him; he'd hide in the hallway's shadows and leap onto my soon-to-be mother's legs, clawing just enough to ruin her stockings right before she went off to work; and he'd knock over the Crock Pot while the humans were out of the house, devouring the bits of beef and leaving all the vegetables, along with the juice, to stain the floor.

The rottenness was what made Dad love this cat; of all the kitties he'd ever been around, Wheat was his favorite and, three decades later, my father still fondly tells stories of this mean-spirited, conniving cat.

There is, however, one exception. Dad has never told me the story about Wheat's revenge. Mom is the one who regales family and friends with this tale whenever the subject of mean kitties comes up, as Dad refuses to talk about it.

Dad was in the habit, every Friday, of mixing a special treat for his cat. This involved wet cat food, dry cat food, a little tuna fish, and some powdered milk. Wheat adored this once-weekly feast and, somehow, knew when it was Friday. Every Friday, when Dad came home from work, the housecat was sitting on the kitchen counter, waiting for his servant to put down his briefcase and start mixing the meal.

One Friday, my father walked into the house and merely said hello to Wheat, who was sitting on the counter as usual. The cat attempted to get Dad's attention several times that afternoon and evening, doing everything from jumping on his lap to standing in front of him and screaming as loudly as possible. At one point, Wheat even jumped up on Dad's lap, put his front paws on the human's shoulders, and meowed in his face, rancid cat breath and all. Dad's week had been long, though. He was more tired than usual that Friday, so he simply forgot Wheat was supposed to get his special treat.

That night, Dad got into bed, leaving Wheat to consume the boring, dry food that was standard the other six days a week. Mom, not being directly involved in Wheat's weekly feast, had no idea Dad had forgotten; she assumed the cat had been annoying the last several hours simply because this was what Wheat did.

This was early spring in South Texas, so my parents slept under just the sheet; Dad, shirtless, had the edge pulled up to his chest and was sleeping on his back.

Sometime during the night, Mom smelled fresh cat crap. She opened one eye, sniffed the air, and realized that this smelly mess was close—very close.

Without moving—Wheat had been around for a few years at this point, so she'd learned to be cautious when there was kitty crap involved—she looked around to see if the cat had done his business near the bed. That was atypical of Wheat, but one never knew what the cat would think of next; it seemed like this housecat was constantly evolving, executing more-nefarious plots.

She turned her head, ever so slightly, and saw Wheat's giant, muted butt, poised mere inches from my father's nose. The cat was frozen on Dad's chest, taking a hellacious dump right in the concave impression of his sternum. Naturally, Wheat's ass was turned toward my father so that the sleeping man could get an eyeful of chocolate starfish if he woke. However, Dad continued sleeping, although nobody's sure how he managed that.

When Wheat finished crapping and hopped off Dad's chest, Mom whispered, "Gary. Wake up. But do not move."

"Huh?"

"Don't move."

"Wha?"

"Wheat took a shit on your chest."

Dad opened his eyes and slowly moved his head downward.

"Oh, shit!"

Wheat had, somehow, managed to crap not directly on my father's chest, but on the sheet. With careful, slow movements, my dad got out from underneath the pile without befouling himself. Wheat sat in the doorway, watching the action and licking one of his front paws. Mom was too busy laughing to help Dad change the sheets.

The next morning, Dad went to the calendar in the kitchen with a red marker and circled every Friday through the end of December.

HOUSESITTING

David McElhinny

AT THE AGE OF SIXTEEN, my friend was going on a two-week vacation and his family asked me if I would look after their house for them. They had three large dogs and a couple of cats. My job would be to stop over twice a day, let the dogs out to pee, feed the various critters and generally look after the house.

I took my task very seriously, knowing how much they loved their animals and home.

Well, on just the second day, I showed up to the house and the second I walked in the door, I could smell it. A nasty, foul stench permeated the home. I let two of the three dogs out, but was unable to find an ancient golden retriever named Sonny. I looked all around, finally finding him hiding behind a large chair in the living room. He had no poker face at all—he was obviously the culprit.

So, like a bloodhound, I began searching the home for the source of the stench, which got stronger as I ascended the stairs. I finally found it in one of the upstairs bedrooms. It was a shimmering pile of poop, two feet in diameter, not quite a solid, not quite a liquid, but something in between. My 10th grade biology teacher Mrs. Garner would have classified it as a colloid. The stink emanating from it was like something not of this Earth. To this day, I have convinced myself that I could actually see the hazy odor hanging in the air like some sort of evil brownish fog.

To make matters worse, this was before the days of central air conditioning, and it was 90-plus degrees that day, about as hot as it ever gets in Western Pennsylvania. I was wearing only a pair of shorts and high-top Nikes.

Knowing that I couldn't simply leave this fermenting pile of foulness for twelve more days, I went to the garage in search of some tools to handle this job. I ultimately found a pair of rubber dishwashing gloves and two, large, industrial-sized dustpans. It could work. It had to!

I trudged back upstairs, armed for the task. I began by trying to slide the dustpans under the gelatinous pile of recycled Alpo. A slurping sound accompanied my efforts as I lifted the edges of it. As if the horrible stench wasn't bad enough before, disturbing this unnatural substance released another level of horror that caused me to begin dry heaving, forcing me to seek refuge across the hall, in my friend's bedroom. Several repeated attempts garnered the same results, ending with me hightailing it out of the room, eyes watering, salivating, trying desperately to keep from vomiting.

It was becoming perfectly clear I was not equipped to handle this situation. So I stood, perplexed, in my friend's bedroom, afraid to venture back across the hall where the mass lay in wait. As I absently looked around the room, I saw salvation, hanging on the bedpost. It was a full gorilla mask, something that had been there for as long as I'd known this family. My mind started calculating the possibilities. I grabbed the simian head, pulling it on like a helmet. The scent inside smelled strongly of rubber and fake fur. This could provide the proper insulation for the task at hand.

At this point, perhaps to give you a better visual, I should explain my teenage physique. Standing six feet, five inches and weighing in the neighborhood of 170 pounds, I looked like some sort of pale grasshopper with acne. X-rays had more meat on their bones than I did.

So I re-entered the spare bedroom, yellow dishwashing gloves pulled up to my bony elbows, armed with white pooper-scoopers in each hand, and a furry, ferocious-looking, black, gorilla mask on my head. I approached the steaming, abhorrent excrement, quickly sliding the dustpans under each side, a gurgling, slurping, sucking sound coming from the beast. After numerous attempts, I finally shoveled under this entity, having to shake it several times to get all of it onto the pans. The mask was doing its job, but the pungent odor was beginning to permeate through, creating a mixed scent of industrial rubber and dog turd. I turned, careful not to drop any of it, and headed for the door. Halfway down the hallway, I began to gag, but there was no turning back, so I hastened my stride to get to the staircase. Part way down the stairs, I began to throw up in my mouth, just a little, my stomach convulsing and spasming as the stench had now overtaken the defense of the mask. I began to run, taking the final eight steps two at a time. I raced through the downstairs and, with a kick of the screen door, I emerged onto the front porch. I hustled down a couple more steps, into the front lawn where I flung the poop into the air, the smell of dog crap drifting away, replaced by the scent of victory.

There I stood, wearing tight, John Stockton-style basketball shorts, dustpans out to the sides, gorilla mask on my head, breathing heavily, bent over at the waist. When I stood up, there, standing in the yard next door, was an old man and his wife. Apparently, they had been doing some gardening, but now, they both stood, mouths agape, looking at this fool in the middle of their neighbors' yard.

I should have gone over, took the mask off, and explained the situation. That's what I should have done. But at 16, I wasn't a great orator. Instead I turned and ran back into the house, where the two other dogs met me at the door. I ushered them inside, shut the door, and stayed hidden, peeking out periodically, waiting for the old couple to finally go inside.

I waited for what seemed like hours before they finally went inside. I then snuck out of the house, jumped in my car and escaped the ugly scene.

But alas, that was not the end of the story.

Two weeks later, when the family returned home from vacation, I stopped by to see how their trip was. The family stood, strangely quiet, looking at me with suspicion. The neighbors had spilled the beans.

It took some time to tell the whole tale as they laughed and mocked me. I explained that me running around their yard with dustpans and a gorilla mask was not the actions of a drug addicted teen crying out for help, but that of a dork trying to perform an exorcism of sorts.

To this day, I can't watch *Planet of the Apes* without getting a whiff of dog crap.

OH, LA MERDE

G. Cornelius

I FIND MYSELF THINKING ABOUT A TOILET.

This is not the toilet of the "Incident," the one recounted in this remembrance—especially because that storied event of my life did not actually occur in, on, or for that matter anywhere *near* a toilet. It's just that as I type that word—*merde*—my mind wanders effortlessly, if aimlessly, back to France, back to the scene of my story and, indeed, the scene of many stories of my youth. Well, at least one particular wayward summer of it. France. That's all I can think to say, as if this one word, this one place name, should satisfy you, as if to hear the word "France" is to understand, scratch your head, smile in musing indulgence, and say, oh so softly, "Ah, yes."

But this is absurd! Absurd that I should imagine any reader capable of making the same imaginative leaps that I have—and still do—when it comes to those words, when it comes to *merde*, to France. And it's absurd to note that France—majestic, romantic, historic France—makes me think of a toilet. But it's true. *Merde* invokes a toilet to me—and not just any toilet, but a specific toilet, the toilet in the men's bathroom at the restaurant *La Carlotta* in Caen, Normandy. Why am I remembering this toilet? Because it was the coolest thing I had ever seen in my life. After one did what one does in the bathroom, the seat retracted into the wall, where it was washed off, disinfected, and then returned, smelling faintly of cleaning fluid and still just a little bit wet to the touch of the back of my thighs. It was very high-tech and robotic, and I could imagine the toilet seat turning vicious, like they do in the movies, grabbing me and either squeezing the life out of me or holding me firm, my pants around my ankles, and flinging the door wide for all to gawk at, point at, and laugh at. This toilet scared me. And yet, I was fascinated; drunk off my ass, I knelt on the stall floor and watched the arms go back into the wall again and again and again, tittering but fearful, until one of my dining companions ferreted me out and dragged me back for the next course.

France is not just a toilet, though, at least not always, a statement in itself both preposterous and telling. France was so much more than that to me: grandeur, spectacle, possibility, love.

It was the summer of my youth, six weeks spent abroad between junior and senior years of college, a time and place where I grew up, where I matured. France was where I ended and began, where my life story stopped and started anew, my metaphoric death and resurrection. I came home a new person—even my mother said so. And yet, somehow, when I look back, when I think of France, for reasons that will soon become quite clear, all I can think of is shit.

Well, *merde*. *Merde* is better. Sounds better. As a word, it's much more pleasing to the American ear. In the French tongue, *merde* has a horrific connotation—to them, the word sounds like... well, it sounds like shit. To us? It's not so bad. *Merde*. Sounds like a horse. Or maybe the nickname for a particularly uptight friend. But a pile of shit? Naah. Doesn't sound like that.

And yet a pile of shit is really what this sordid tale is all about. And it's why, regardless of how much my entire time abroad impacted me, when I think of France, I think of poo. I can't help it. Like Pavlov's dog, when I hear a trilled "r" or the opening strains of "La Marseillaise," I clutch my stomach in conditioned response.

It wasn't my fault. I'd like to state that for the record, because, as you'll read, it really, truly, and wholly *was* my fault. But no one warned me about France. Oh sure, I thought I was ready for how different things would be over there. I thought I was amply prepared. And for the most part, I was. I was prepared for the frostiness, prepared for the fact that people stared openly at anyone who looked—well, who looked *un*French—prepared for the fact that the people were often combative, rude, or just plain dismissive. I suppose I shouldered some of the blame for this. I was just a small-town American college student, a rube with a backpack and two years of college French. I looked American; I sounded American; hell, I even smelled American (mostly because I bathed every day.) In a small provincial city I stood out like a big, sore, red-white-and-blue thumb. So it was no surprise that some people took their time to warm up to me.

But I was ready for that. That was easy to deal with. I quickly learned that buying a Frenchman a drink made him your bosom companion, at least for an hour or so, and that arguing—combative debate, really—is just a common pastime among young people there. I learned that staring at someone openly and brazenly really should be interpreted as a compliment, and I learned to appreciate such compliments at least seven times a day. I adjusted. I got by. Hell, I thrived. I got used to all that.

What I didn't get used to was the toilet situation.

France is a country with a dearth of toilets. There was, when I was there, a serious shortage of public restroom facilities. Now, I was a healthy, hungry, typically overweight American college student with an appetite for fried foods and anything with cheese. The end result of a lifetime of continually breaking one of the seven deadly sins was that I had become as regular as the rising sun. Greenwich Mean Time could set its clocks by the movements of my bowel. Amongst the members of my family I had elevated the concept of the "appointment shit" to an art form. Post-breakfast, mid-afternoon, after-dinner; no matter where I was or what I ate, my three times a day habit came forth as natural and insistent as a door-to-door Bible salesman. So it did not matter that I was in a foreign land; shit will out.

Post-breakfast and after-dinner were not a problem for me. Both found me in my campus housing and within striking distance of the antiquated pull toilets (two for eighty residents of the floor) that, coincidentally or not, were located across the hall from my dorm room (apparently, just as I had been warned about the French, the French had been warned about me.) But that mid-afternoon shit—coming along right at 4:00 sharp—that was the problem. I never knew where I was going to be. As part of my program, I went on excursions three or four times a week. These were amazing trips—Mont St. Michel, Le Mans, a vineyard and orchard that specialized in fruit wines—at 4:00 on any given day I could be studying in my dorm room, playing soccer on the quad, riding in a bus, climbing seven stories to a medieval chapel, or out in the middle of a field admiring apple trees. Yet regardless, at 4:00, I needed to shit. And with my bowel, this regular appointment is never a negotiation. There is no back and forth between me and my ass, trying to buy some extra time. There's typically a warning shot across the bow, letting me know what is coming; if that is ignored, then come the belly cramps, the hunched form, and the mad dash for relief. If *that* is ignored—well, let's just say I was never foolish enough to ignore that first warning shot. I knew that when my body told me it was time to go, it wasn't kidding.

The problem wasn't me—the problem was France. In America, public parks always have a bathroom. In fact, there are public restrooms everywhere, for all the other four o'clockers like me. This was not so in France. In France, restrooms were few and far between. And sometimes downright odd. And usually hard to find. Even in a mall—a big, brand-spanking-new expansive shopping mall—the crapper could be difficult to locate. My second day in France I had to make a mad dash into a ladies' room just to avoid the 4:00 rush in my pants. Fortunately, there was no one in the bathroom when I entered, though I caused some mild distress amongst three old biddies fixing their hair and adjusting their support hose when I slunk back out.

But the worst 4:00 situation occurred in a tiny town somewhere outside the walled village of St. Malo. I always took responsibility for my shit. I did my best to ascertain where I was going to be at any given 4:00, just to make sure I'd have somewhere to go. This particular day, we were supposed to arrive back at university housing at exactly 4:00. It was going to be close, and I'd probably have to run up the three flights to my floor with my butt muscles clenched in that awkward, leggy, ostrich-like dash that people in desperate need of a toilet sometimes get, but I could do it.

Unfortunately, the bus broke down. And there we were, in a village of maybe less than three hundred people, and I had to shit. We'd been told to wander around the town and soak in the local color while the bus driver fixed the problem. I'd been wandering for about twenty minutes when it hit me. Uh-oh. Warning shot. Not much time now. I knew that there was no bathroom on the bus, so I looked for someplace—anyplace— where I could take a shit. Time was of the essence. There. A restaurant. Well, a bar. Well, a dive. No matter. It was the only public facility in the entire town that I could readily identify. It would have to do.

Later in life, the professor in me who sometimes teaches linguistics would become fascinated that there, tucked away in some remote corner of the Brittany region in northwestern France, I had stumbled across a group of individuals who still spoke in the Breton Gaelic language and not French. This was a rare privilege, to hear native speakers of a language that was rapidly dying out. It is a memory that, as an intellectual and professor, I have long treasured and shared with my own students. At the moment, however, the guttural subtleties of the Breton tongue were lost on me. I had to shit. I had to shit now. And the fact that these people were so damned Breton meant that we could not understand each other. My schoolboy French was laughable to them, and their accent was so thick, so rough and raucous, that nothing they said made sense to me. I did the best I could. Clutching my ass, I gave the universal sign for having to go to the bathroom—I did a shit dance. The bartender seemed to finally understand, and pointed down a dim hallway with his thumb.

There was a door. Thank heavens. Relief. I opened it. A small hallway. Then stairs going down. Cursing, I took them two at a time. I found myself in a large basement, dimly lit, musty, and labyrinthine. There had to be a toilet somewhere. I went around one corner, two, trying to find something—somewhere—I could take a dump. One dead end led to another. Then my nose detected the sweet scent of unflushed piss. I turned one more corner and spied, off to the left, a sink. And there, next to the sink, was a hole in the ground.

What the fuck? I had never seen anything like this in my life. The hole was built directly into the ground right next to a large utensil sink. It contained some sort of cracked porcelain basin—the color of piss, I musingly noted—and there, in the middle, a dank, dark hole that reeked of sewage. I had heard of stand-up toilets, places where you literally pissed into a hole in the ground, but I had thought those an archaic product of yesteryear, like oil lamps or thank-you notes. I couldn't believe my luck—the one public toilet in this entire godforsaken hole of a town had originated sometime in the late nineteenth century. Great. Here was my chance to shit in a piece of history and yet, somehow, I found the awe of the moment lacking.

Still, my bowel would not be denied. What choice did I have? And yet I was uneasy. There was no door here, no walls, no separate room. The sink and hole were wide open to the entire cellar. If anyone were to walk in, they'd see... well, they'd see me in repose, that's what they'd see. In the end, though, none of it mattered. It couldn't matter—it was 4:00. I had no choice. Positioning my feet on either side of the hole, I lowered my pants and assumed a squatting position.

I began to shit.

For a brief moment, I wondered if this was how women were purported to have given birth in the Middle Ages, squatting in the fields and then picking up the baby and getting back to work. Those thoughts flew from my head the moment the smell hit me. There was precious little water in that hole, and my shit hit the muck-covered floor with a sickening plop that curdled my stomach and threatened to raise the bile out of my gullet and onto the floor in front of me. I couldn't believe those happy, wine-drinking Bretons upstairs did this everyday. I did my best to distract my mind from my unhappy circumstances, but there was little else to focus on save this particular moment in my life. Like all red-blooded American males, normally when I shit, I read. I've been known to get through an entire *People* magazine in an outing, with time to muse about who truly is best dressed and not. Here I had nothing to do but squat and pray that no one else needed to use the loo until I was done.

Finally, the last bit of lunch slithered out of me and into the hole below. I looked around for some toilet paper. They had none. Of course not. There was an old, grease-covered rag on the sink. Fuck it. I took the rag and did the best I could. Disgusted, I tossed that into the hole as well.

I stood back to admire my handiwork. I have to say that, for a first-timer, I had pretty decent aim. Almost all of it went into the hole. But the stench was so strong, it would have killed cancer. I needed to flush. There was a little pull cord next to the sink. I reached over and pulled it. Nothing happened. I did it again. Still nothing. I did it a third time. As I pulled again, this time, something did happen.

The door to the cellar opened.

It was a large, heavy, rickety door, and I heard it open faintly. I also heard a nearly imperceptible buzzing sound in the distance. With a rush of clarity I could only describe as being filled with utter dread, it suddenly dawned on me that this particular pull cord was, in fact, *not* designed to flush the toilet. It was part of an antiquated communications system. It let the people upstairs know that someone downstairs needed them. In this case, it let them know that *I* needed them.

Clarity is a funny thing. Sometimes, when you suddenly understand one thing that is puzzling you, you understand a great many other things, too. For example: seconds after I realized that the pull cord was not designed to flush the toilet I likewise realized that the hole in the floor was not designed to shit in. In fact, it wasn't a toilet at all. It was simply a drainage grate. Just a hole that every basement has to drain off any excess water that seeps in from flooding during heavy rainstorms. And look, yes, right there next to the sink—the grated cover for the hole that someone had absent-mindedly neglected to replace. It smelled of dank water and old pipe. Turns out it didn't really smell of old piss and shit at all.

At least, not until now.

So there I was. An American twenty-one-year-old college student in a small bar somewhere deep in the heart of Brittany in a basement room with a group of burly, surly Breton men coming down to get me, and I have just taken a big shit in what is essentially the middle of the floor. I rather suspected that this scenario would somehow end with me getting a few black eyes and broken limbs. So I did what any bold, hotheaded masculine youth would do—I hid.

I waited behind a corner until the two men coming into the basement veered off in the opposite direction. Then, as quickly and quietly as possible, I hastened up the stairs. As I reached the door I heard a loud exclamation of what I was pretty sure was ample parts surprise and disgust, though I did not stick around to find out exactly what the men were saying. As I passed through the dim hallway and back into the bar I noticed a small door on my left that I had not spied coming through the first time. I paused for just a second to glance inside. Yup. The toilet.

Discretion is often the better part of valor. I beat a hasty retreat and was elated to find that the bus was repaired and we were ready to be underway. As we pulled out I imagined a group of Breton townsfolk with pitchforks and torches chasing after the bus, demanding that I be left behind to face village justice. But luckily for me, I managed to escape unscathed.

Well, I escaped unscathed physically. Psychologically is another matter. For now, every time I think of France, I think of shit. No matter the amazing adventures I had there, no matter what I learned or how I changed and grew, no matter what happened, whenever anyone mentions France, I involuntarily think of that little hole-in-the-wall bar and that little hole in the basement floor. I sometimes wonder if they still talk about the crazy American who defiled their drainage system. I wonder if every Fourth of July they curse the notion that their country ever gave ours the Statue of Liberty, or if apple pies are burned in the street in protest. I guess I'll never know. Still, France will always be connected with shit for me. Well, *merde*. Connected to *merde*. Perhaps if I can remember that French word, *merde*, then maybe, just maybe, it'll get better.

After all, shit just sounds better in French.

MY LIFE IN POO:
A RETROSPECTIVE

Melinda J. Combs

July 22, 1969

My brother, age two, yanks off his dirty diaper, then paints bedroom walls and bed with poo art. Me: sleeping. My mother: out of the house, running errands. My father: supposedly babysitting, probably asleep. He wakes up, discovers new decor, throws everything away. My mother retrieves sheets, clothes and teddy bear from trash to clean. Doesn't bode well for future.

August 2, 1974

Depart for hike in southern Oregon wilds with my father. Thirty feet from cabin, Dad stops suddenly. Bends over a pile of bear shit, then pokes a stick in it. He reports, "It's steaming. We need to go back inside. NOW." Look of concern on his face tells me to obey. For a change.

May 1, 1983

High school lunch: friends and I are on our way to cars, walking into the school parking lot. Everyone is there, meandering around, trying to find cars, friends, paramours. Hot liquid hits my face, especially left eye and lips. I ask, "What the hell was that?" Friends scatter, yelling, pointing, "A bird just shit on you!" Only one friend stays, grabs Kleenex out of her purse (she was always motherly, even in high school), and starts to clean me up. In the bathroom, we look in the mirror and see seagull shit spattered across me: from my hair to my shirt. Spend a frantic half an hour under the faucet in various positions. I'm still worried I swallowed seagull shit.

January 15, 1987

My soon-to-be stepmom is constipated for over a week, so takes a handful of laxatives. They finally work while she's driving home after getting into a fight with my father. The stress causes her to shit pants while seated in yellow Cadillac. Poo rises above the waistband of her jeans, spreads onto pleather. She recounts story, laughing.

March 27, 1989

Spend semester abroad. See my first U.S.S.R. toilet. A hole in a tiled floor. Nowhere to sit. Nothing to hold onto. Decide to shit outside instead.

April 2, 1989

Still on semester abroad. Visit India and take showers with a washrag in mouth to avoid tainted water, yet still come down with diarrhea for rest of trip.

June 27, 1991

Making out on a southern California beach with random guy I met in downtown bar. Friend and I run off to pee in sand. I poo instead. Guy asks what took so long: I tell a lie.

March 27, 1992

Make up a song for my yellow lab, Chief. Part of the lyrics: "If I were a doggy, I'd want to be you cuz I'd get to go poo outside." My favorite line of the song.

October 18, 1993
Diagnosed with Hepatitis A. I turn yellow and so does my poo.

September 1, 1994
Buy the book *Everyone Poops* for same friend who saved me from seagull shit to read to her kindergarten class. She reports back to me, "When I finished it, my students started to chant, 'Even Mrs. Delmarco poops.'" She never reads book to kindergarten class again.

October 24, 1994
Belly finally recovers from dysentery I got in India. Yes. Five years. Really.

August 1, 1995
Go on outdoor leadership program for 10-days in Joshua Tree. Carry own water. No showers. Learn how to dig holes to shit in, then cover holes. Have to carry out dirty toilet paper. Start wiping ass with rocks. Much easier. Feels more adventurous.

June 12, 1998
Childhood friend gets married. My fiancé and I drink way too much at wedding. After wedding, fiancé commandeers bathroom. As usual. Can't wait, so I shit outside the hotel room, hidden in the bushes, still in bridesmaid dress. Never tell fiancé. Leave bridesmaid dress in hotel closet. On purpose. Can't bear to wear it again.

April 11, 2000
Come down with worst flu of life. Doctor wants fecal sample to run tests. Instructed to buy a clear casserole-sized Pyrex dish to put inside of toilet. Shit in Pyrex, grab samples. Afterward, fiancé wraps returned container in towels and

throws into community trash bin. Am told that means true love.

January 5, 2003

Drop keys in toilet after taking dump in Target restroom. Retrieve keys with hands as last resort. Run hands and keys under scalding water. Never look at keys the same again. Never shit at Target again. Wash hands over and over again.

June 15, 2005

Travel to Cuba, legally, to study birds. Live in tent for two weeks. Filthy toilet in nearby reserve house unexpectedly loses toilet seat. Completely MIA. Probably used to fix broken jeep. Use toilet a few times without toilet seat. Doesn't work well: rim is too narrow to sit on comfortably. Decide to shit outside, illegally, for rest of trip. Use leaves and rocks again.

June 27, 2009

Live in dorm (again at age forty) for a weeklong workshop class. Can't comfortably poo with other participants nearby. Think that I may not shit all week. Am reminded by friend at workshop, "Everybody's in the same boat." Still not convinced. I get up at 4AM to take dump when everyone is still asleep. Realize that I hate dorm living.

April 11, 2010

Am asked to contribute piece to friend's shit anthology. Email parents asking for more information on brother's diaper incident for anthology. Ask parents if they are proud of me and where my writing career is going. They don't answer.

CODE BROWN

ABOUT THE CONTRIBUTORS

Garrett Calcaterra is an author of dark speculative fiction, as well as a humorist. His books include *Dreamwielder, Umbral Visions, The Roads to Baldairn Motte* and *A Good Brew is Hard to Find*, a humorous choose-your-own-adventure style speculative fiction novel. You can learn more about his writing at www.garrettcalcaterra.com

Jeffrey Wallace lives, writes, and teaches in Orange County, CA. His short stories and humorous essays have appeared in a variety of magazines, newspapers, and short story anthologies.

Lisa Hallsted grew up in Orange County, California and received her bachelors in English Literature from Loma Linda University. She is currently working on a travel memoir about a road trip across America she took with her brother.

Shannon Medisky is a leading expert in how to fail, how to be wrong the right way and how to effectively navigate the unknown, even when it's—well—icky! Her mission is to help kids put fear and failure in their place; in the right perspective, so that they can ultimately succeed. Her articles have been featured in many prominent magazines such as *Exceptional Parents, Adoptive Families, Hybrid Mom, Mothering* and Focus on the Family's *Thriving Family*.

Michael Williams has lived in the rural West for 30 years where he has been a park ranger, country singer, social critic, and museum exhibitionist. In other times and places he recorded Costa Rican calypso music, worked with Galapagos tortoises, redecorated a botanical garden in Honduras, and was blockaded in Bolivia. In his spare time he reads, writes, explores desert cliff dwellings, and studies the human race.

Eric Scot Tryon has lived and shat all over the great state of California. He has published a dozen short stories in various literary magazines and anthologies such as *Glimmer Train* and *Willow Springs*. And while this is his first venture into non-fiction, his friend Jeremy often wishes this story was indeed, just a product of imagination.

John Fox has traveled to more than 40 countries around the globe and taught composition and literature at 5 universities in Southern California. His writing credits include *PBS Online*, the *Los Angeles Times*, *US Airways Magazine*, *The Writer Magazine*, and *Fieldstone Review*. He currently lives in Orange County and has newborn twin sons, which allows him to explore entirely new territories of poop.

Bob Jere is the drummer in a prominent southern rock band. In addition, he is a drum instructor and the author of numerous books and magazine columns on drumming. He has toured (and pooped) all over the world, and no, his name isn't really Bob Jere.

Daniel A. Roberts lives in Oklahoma City with his wife and two teenage daughters. Having spent the majority of his life living in Florida, Daniel doesn't regret relocating to the mid-west, where the seasonal changes are slow, sweet and relaxing. While his CNA days are long gone in real life, he continues to write in the realms of Science Fiction and Fantasy. His work can be easily found in any online retailer.

Holly Vance has always been a storyteller. In her elementary years, she was asked to tell ghost stories at slumber parties; in the 8th grade, she wrote her first short story, "The Castle;" and in high school, she wrote her first novel. Even though a career assessment test indicated Holly might do well in the FBI, she chose to go into teaching. While enlightening students' minds, Holly has written two more novels: a romance and a crime thriller. She has enjoyed some success with the publication of a vampire short story and by gaining a following at her blog The Genres of My Life. Blogging has developed Holly's skills for humor writing and language analysis, resulting in the publication of several essays on modern day slang in online journals.

Sarah Marie is a full-time grad student and writer currently enjoying life in Kentucky. She occasionally posts something interesting at http://beerachick.com/.

David McElhinny is a novelist who lives near Pittsburgh, Pennsylvania. with his wife and two children. His current novels include *Zero*, *Signs of Life* and *Storm*.

G. Cornelius. Since his days of more youthful indiscretions, G. Cornelius has lost fifty pounds and no longer dreads 4:00. Further details of his biography remain scant since, unsurprisingly, he feels that, in this case, discretion remains the better part of valor, in order to avoid further possible international incident.

Melinda J. Combs lives in Southern California where she's trying to find the meaning of life. In the meantime, she's been published in *Gargoyle*, *Barely South Review*, *Far From Home: Father-Daughter Travel Adventures*, and *Women's Best Friend*. She also co-authored the book, *In Service to the Mouse*, with former Disney executive, Jack Lindquist. Find her on Twitter: @LittleMighty.

Made in the USA
Lexington, KY
18 December 2018